Gary,

Congratulations on that South Dallas listing.

This will be your greatest year yet, and your future looks even better. It's a pleasure working with you.

Teresa Gary

TEN GREATEST SALESPERSONS

Books by Robert L. Shook

WINNING IMAGES

HOW TO BE THE COMPLETE PROFESSIONAL SALESMAN
(with Herbert Shook)

TOTAL COMMITMENT
(with Ronald Bingamen)

Ten Greatest Salespersons

What They Say About Selling

ROBERT L. SHOOK

1817

HARPER & ROW, PUBLISHERS

New York, Hagerstown, San Francisco, London

Portions of this work originally appeared in *Success Unlimited* magazine.

Designed by Eve Callahan

Library of Congress Cataloging in Publication Data

Shook, Robert L.   1938–
    Ten greatest salespersons.
    1. Sales personnel—United States—Interviews.
2. Selling. I. Title.
HF5439.5.S46 1978   658.85   78-2165
ISBN 0-06-014012-7

79 80 81 82 10 9 8 7 6 5 4 3 2

To Bobbie, with love

Acknowledgments

To my publisher, Irv Levey, who planted the seed and whose advice I sought during the entire writing of the manuscript. I am also grateful to Anne Forster, who helped me prepare the manuscript, and to Nancy Cone, who edited the manuscript. I also thank the following people for their contributions: Bob Binstock, Noel Black, Jr., Joyce Darveau, Earl Dobert, Mike Frank, Tom Hingson, Dale Hvizak, Ron Karp, Patricia Lewis, William Magel, Jerry Maxwell, Sig Munster, H. Jackson Pontius, Jerry Schottenstein, Arthur Shapiro, Herb Shook, Dorothy Snow, Andrew Staursky, Geraldine Ulmer, and Jon Woods.

Contents

TEN GREATEST SALESPERSONS

Introduction

The *salesman* in me has a great urge to begin this introduction with a hard-hitting sales presentation. But the *author* in me keeps suggesting that I stay quiet and let the ten people I'm about to introduce take over. By letting *them* make the presentation, I will have the greatest sales organization in America representing my cause. Under these circumstances it would be presumptuous for me to interfere.

Briefly, here are ten of America's greatest salespersons, in the order that they were interviewed for this book. Because they came across as informal people, my introductions will be equally informal.

ˋ First, you will meet a dynamic guy named *Joe Girard,* the number one automobile and truck salesman in the world. I am speaking about retail sales, or as Joe puts it, "belly-to-belly selling." He's the only salesman to have ever been written up in *The Guinness Book of World Records.* During the past eleven years, Joe has consistently sold more than twice as many cars as whoever happened to be the number two car salesperson.

Joe Gandolfo, the number one life insurance agent in the world, has been averaging approximately $800 million in sales a year, and in 1975, his biggest year, he sold more than a billion dollars' worth. That's like breaking the three-minute mile. Joe's earnings may well be the highest of any salesperson in America.

Next we have a lovely and talented woman, *Bernice Hansen,* who has been with Amway Corporation since its early days, when it consisted of only ten to twelve salespersons. Bernice started an Amway distributorship with her late husband, Fred, and their family business now consists of an estimated 130,000 distributorships.

Handsome *Buck Rodgers* looks more like a matinee idol than the vice president of marketing for IBM. As the company's worldwide sales manager, Buck heads a sales organization made up of more than 70,000 people!

Shelby Carter is the senior vice president of Xerox in charge of U.S. field operations. Without a doubt, Shelby is the most enthusiastic, hard-hitting sales manager I have ever met. With leaders like him, it is no wonder Xerox has a reputation for being one of the world's finest marketing organizations.

From the size of him, *Rich Port* might be a former NFL linebacker. He happens to be the founder and chairman of the board of perhaps America's largest residential real estate firm. Rich's organization consists of 375 salespersons and has twenty-five offices in the Greater Chicago area, with two more to be opened very soon.

A vigorous and delightful lady, *Edna Larsen* represents Avon in North St. Paul, Minnesota, There are approximately 975,000 Avon Representatives throughout the world, and Edna is at the very top.

Enthusiastic *Martin Shafiroff* is a stockbroker with Lehman Brothers Kuhn Loeb, Inc., in New York City. He generates about $1.5 million each year in commissions and is generally recognized as the top producer in the retail end of the securities business.

The distinguished-looking *Mike Curto* is group vice president of US Steel Corporation. He heads the steel division, which accounts for approximately 75 percent of the corporation's $9 billion in annual sales and revenues.

Finally, there is energetic *Bill Bresnan,* who is president of the nation's largest operator of cable television systems, Teleprompter's cable television division.

I should explain how these ten individuals were selected to be included in *Ten Greatest Salespersons*. First, it is important to realize that all ten began their careers in sales. When a salesperson excels in some industries, such as real estate, insurance, or securities, his or her outstanding sales production does not necessarily warrant a promotion into management. The rewards usually come in the form of higher commissions, and often a top producer can generate higher annual earnings than the board chairmen and presidents of most major American corporations. On the other hand, with companies like IBM, Xerox, US Steel, and Teleprompter, a top salesperson will generally seek managerial opportunities for advancement, so at a certain career point, he or she will no longer continue to sell in the field on a daily basis. In yet other industries, a top salesperson has an option either to remain in the field *or* be promoted into management; each offers a fine opportunity. I stress this point because *Ten Greatest Salespersons* includes individuals who have excelled in selling in a variety of businesses, and, in each case, the person has reached the pinnacle of success in his or her respective field.·

I spent many hours researching every major industry so that I could properly select the right people for this book. Admittedly, Joe Gandolfo's reputation in the insurance industry had already established him as the number one life insurance agent in the world, and likewise Joe Girard, the world's greatest automobile and truck salesman, was an easy choice. Martin Shafiroff has more recently established himself as the nation's number one retail stockbroker. On the other hand, several individuals throughout the country were candidates for the residential real estate salesperson. It was Rich Port's superior performance over the past quarter of a century that influenced my final decision. I wasn't interested in flashes in the pan who may have been superstars for a year or two but faded, perhaps as a result of a short-term economic slump. Therefore, one of my most important criteria was *tenure*.

In other instances, I chose the leading company within a particular industry. Thus, in the computer field, IBM was an obvious choice; so was Xerox in copying and duplicating equipment, Teleprompter in cable television, US Steel in heavy industry, Avon in cosmetics, and Amway in personal care and household products. Once I had selected the company, I communicated directly with its public relations department, and they named an obvious candidate. However, when I contacted Avon and Amway, each had a handful of outstanding candidates. Upon receiving data on the "nominated" individuals, I carefully studied each person's qualifications and arrived at a final decision.

Depending upon the organization of the company, *Ten Greatest Salespersons* includes both personal producers and sales executives. As I previously stated, I wanted to include in this book only the most outstanding salespersons. But in some cases, the individual I wanted was no longer involved in day-to-day selling activities; he had been promoted to an executive position. It is important to understand, however, that excellence in salesmanship had earned his promotion, and furthermore, although he was at a higher level, selling was still the most basic part of his present position.

I don't doubt that some readers will disagree with my selections. They will say that I should have included a salesperson in some other industry; if I had followed such advice, I would have ended up writing an encyclopedia instead of a single book. Space limitations restricted me to ten selections, and giving the book the right balance was more important than increasing the number of salespersons. But I defy anyone to assemble a team of ten individuals with a better overall track record than those here included.

Ten Greatest Salespersons is not based on theory. Too many books have been published that speculate on how a salesperson should react in a hypothetical situation. Many have been written by salesmen with limited points of view, or by authors who have never sold anything—except manuscripts.

As author, I don't claim the credit for the ideas and concepts expressed by these ten super producers. I simply tape-recorded interviews with each of them, and my work was more like editing than creative writing. I cross-examined each individual so that I could dig into *why* he does *what* he does. I believe that understanding a concept is vital in order to succeed with its application.

I also set out to disprove once and for all the "natural born salesman" myth. I had always believed that a person is no more naturally born to be a salesperson than to be a dentist, a plumber, or a certified accountant. My personal meetings with each of the individuals in *Ten Greatest Salespersons* supported my contention that selling skills are learned and developed; there is little room for success based on any so-called natural qualities. Perhaps it's possible to be born with a good pitching arm or a natural aptitude to sing country music and to gain success by developing such talents. But selling isn't a talent; it's an ability. It must be acquired and mastered. It depends on a lot more than a nice smile and a gift of gab. The people in this book don't rely solely on their God-given talents. They have achieved success through hard work, dedication, and a professional approach to selling.

As a salesman/author, I want to point out that salespersons are a different breed from ordinary people. While, for example, a football player will accept a coach who has never played football, a salesman will reject a sales manager who doesn't have a proven track record as a leading salesman. For those skeptics, *Ten Greatest Salespersons* is based on the sales experiences of leading sales personalities who are among the most respected and accomplished people in their fields. I believe that this book will have more credibility on the subject of selling than any previous book, not because I am its author, but because it's based on *what great salespeople say about selling.*

By now, you can readily observe that I am very enthusiastic about *Ten Greatest Salespersons.* And for good reason. While it's a lot of work to research each person, travel and interview him or her, transcribe the tapes, and then write the chapter, I received a couple of bonuses which don't normally come from writing a manuscript. First, I met ten highly positive, dynamic people. Their enthusiasm was contagious. As I completed one chapter and went on to the next, I received, in effect, a pep talk that gave me the momentum to continue the project. I kept "peaking" throughout the ten interviews I conducted. Second, as a special bonus, I personally learned a great deal about selling. I must confess this came as a complete surprise! After all, selling has been my entire career, and in many circles I am considered an outstanding salesman. I defy *any* salesperson to state that he or she won't benefit from *Ten Greatest Salespersons*. No salesperson is so good that he or she can't learn from the top sales experts in America.

And I discovered another thing. Most salespeople exchange ideas only with individuals in the same field. Rarely, for example, will an insurance agent exchange ideas with a computer salesman, or a real estate broker talk about selling with a steel salesperson. I am absolutely amazed at the vast knowledge I myself gained by discovering what the top salespersons in industries other than mine are doing, and how easily I can apply their techniques and concepts in my own selling, In fact, I believe that many ideas can be borrowed from another industry and applied to *your* selling after some refinement for your particular situation, and the result may be better than the original idea. Some narrow-minded people may call this copying; I think of it as resourcefulness.

Almost every selling concept in this book can be transplanted to your individual selling field. I purposely avoided technical information so that the techniques and strategies included could benefit all readers. I suggest that you read each chapter thoroughly, and don't be shy about borrowing from each one. The individuals presented here are not only the greatest salespersons I have ever met, but they're also warm, sincere, and humble people. It's with great professional pride that they invite you to share their successful selling concepts. And when you do, you'll be getting your information from the very best available sources.

R. L. S.

1

Joe Girard

(AUTOMOBILES)

"You gotta sell yourself."

· In 1976, for the eleventh consecutive year, Joe Girard sold more automobiles and trucks on a one-to-one basis than anyone else in the world! "All my sales were *retail,*" he states emphatically, "one car at a time. No wholesale or fleet sales are included. That's belly-to-belly selling." No salesman has ever held both the auto and truck world title during the same year. ·

In 1973, Joe sold 1,425 cars and trucks, a world record which may never be broken. Joe is the only salesman listed in the business section of *The Guinness Book of World Records.* It says:

> ι **GREATEST SALESMAN.** The all-time record for automobile salesmanship in individual units sold is 1,425 in 1973 by Joe Girard of Detroit, Michigan, winner of the Number One Car Salesman title every year since 1966. His commissions in 1975 totaled $191,000. ·

During the 1974 Arab oil embargo, his sales totaled 1,376. "This was a 'slump' year for the automotive industry, when everybody was pleading poverty," Joe laughs. His sales during 1975 tallied 1,360, but during that year Detroit went on a five-day work week, and thus became the only major city in the United States not to sell cars on Saturday or Sunday. In 1976, his sales were "only" 1,285, still not bad considering he spent a great deal of his time on speaking engagements and working on his book, *How to Sell Anything to Anybody* (New York, Simon & Schuster, 1978). Joe's 1976 earnings exceeded $200,000.

Joe's achievements have been written up in many national magazines, including *Newsweek, Woman's Day, Successful Meetings, Success Unlimited,* and *Penthouse;* and hundreds of newspapers have acclaimed his sales records. Joe has appeared in dozens of news stories on radio and television, and has made personal appearances on such programs as *To Tell the Truth, What's My Line,* and the *Tomorrow* show.

In 1975, the American Academy of Achievement presented Girard with the Golden Plate Award, an honor bestowed upon a select group of Americans from every walk of life who the Academy believes are "Captains of Achievement." (Other recipients include John K. Jamieson, Exxon Corporation's chairman; Herman Lay, chairman of the board of Pepsi Cola Company; Art Linkletter; Willie Mays; Dr. Werner Von Braun; and Dr. Carl Sagan.)

Joe is also the president of Girard Productions, Inc., a company that produces and markets his sales training films and presents the *Joe Girard Sales Conference,* a sales training program conducted throughout the United States and Canada.

Joe was born on November 1, 1928, to a Sicilian immigrant family on Detroit's lower east side. He quit school in the eleventh grade. Prior to selling cars he was employed as a custom home builder.

Joe and his wife, June, live in Grosse Pointe Shores, an exclusive Detroit suburb. They have a son, Joe, Jr., age twenty-four, who works as Girard's assistant, and a daughter, Grace, age twenty-two, who is an administrative assistant at Girard Productions.

The following figures represent Joe Girard's amazing eleven-year sales production:

YEAR	NUMBER OF CARS AND TRUCKS SOLD
1966	614
1967	667
1968	708
1969	764
1970	843
1971	980
1972	1,208
1973	1,425
1974	1,376
1975	1,360
1976	1,285

JOE GIRARD

When it comes to selling retail cars and trucks, Joe Girard is in a class all by himself. He has sold more retail units than any other person in the world for the past eleven years. (While the final figures for 1977 are not available, it should be noted that a high percentage of his time was spent with other business activities, including speaking engagements, Girard Productions, Inc., and completion of *How to Sell Anything to Anybody.* In spite of these activities, Girard still sold more cars and trucks during 1977 than any other salesperson.) In fact, the number two salesman is never the same person, and Joe will sell more than twice as much as whoever happens to come in in second place! Such a comparison puts his achievement in proper perspective. *His sales are more than double those of the next best automobile salesman in the world.*

What's Joe's great secret that enables him to sell cars and trucks in such record-breaking numbers? What is he doing differently from the hundreds of thousands of other automobile salesmen throughout the world?

- "I have no big secrets which nobody else has." Joe smiles. "I simply sell the world's best product, that's all. *I sell Joe Girard!"* -

It really sounds simple when Joe says, *"You gotta sell your-*

self.'' After all, it's a basic selling philosophy, passed on to every novice salesperson in America during his or her very first day in the field. How many times have we heard that people want to do business with people they like? Why is it, however, that so many salesmen fail to heed this advice?

"I make every customer *want* to do business with me," Joe claims. "From the moment he walks in, I don't care if I haven't seen him for five years, I make him feel like I saw him yesterday, and I really missed him."

"Say, where the hell have you been?" Joe warmly greets the customer as he walks into the showroom.

"Er, well, I haven't needed a car up until now," the customer apologizes.

"D'ya have to need a car just to stop in and say hello when you're passing by? I thought we were friends. You pass by our showroom every day going back and forth to work, old buddy. I want you to stop in and say hello from now on." Joe lowers his voice and bows. "C'mon in my office and tell me about your-self." With his arm over the man's shoulder, Joe leads him to his office.

"You know, sincerity is something which you can't read or let somebody teach you," Joe explains. "You gotta be natural, and do you know what? People like people who are honest. And salesmen gotta be honest and show that they care.

"How many times have you walked out of a restaurant, for example, and said to your wife, 'Honey, remind me never to come in here again, will ya?' Do you know what builds great restaurants? They're built by word of mouth, because people tell other people how much they *cared* for you. The great restaurants in this country have love and care coming out of their kitchens. They have people in the kitchen who are looking out to make sure that the guy in the dining room is going to get a fair shake and a fair deal.

"And when I sell a car, my customer's gonna leave with the same feeling that he'll get when he walks out of a great restau-rant. You know, that satisfied, contented feeling. He's gonna be thinking, That Girard was pretty good to me. I really enjoyed buying a car from him. No kidding. He really made it fun. And I've never had anyone give me a demonstration ride [in Detroit, it is not standard practice for automobile dealers to give demonstration rides]. I've been to nine places, and he's the only guy. By golly, he didn't even ask me. He had the car right there, and told me to get in and try it out.

"You just pull it out and tell the guy to get in," Joe says. "You'd be amazed how surprised the customer is when you insist that he try it out. I tell him, 'Ya wouldn't want to buy anything unless you tried it, would you? Go ahead, take it out,' and I sit him down in the driver's seat. 'D'ya mean you're gonna let me drive a car? Nobody's ever offered before!' 'I wouldn't let you buy anything unless you liked it.'

"Do you want to know what I sell?" Joe again emphasizes. "I sell Joe Girard: *the Greatest Product in the World!*"

Girard understands people, not cars. It just so happens that his product is automobiles.

"I don't know technical knowledge about automobiles. Hell, that's not what they're buying. You'll just scare most of 'em away when you get into gear ratios and horsepower. When a customer asks about them, I say, 'Look, Mr. Jones, I don't know from gear ratios. If you really want me to find out for you I could ask somebody in the back to explain all that. But I don't even know how to put gas in the car. I swear to you. Honest to God! All I know is that I could give you the best service and I could give you the best price. And if I can give you the best service and the best price, you're gonna bring more customers back to me.'

"'Honest to God, product knowledge would drive me nuts. But if you want to know, I could take you to a guy in the back who will be glad to answer your questions,'" Joe cheerfully tells the customer.

"Most salesmen bore a guy to death when they start to talk about the technical details about the car. I've seen salesmen sell a car and then buy it back. I watch these guys and I say to myself, 'He's got the car sold, but he won't shut up. Why don't he just give the customer his pen and tell him to put down his OK on the order pad? What the devil is he trying to prove to the customer, anyhow? Show him how smart he is?'

"You got to qualify your customer. You have to know what makes that guy tick. You know, Joe Louis was my friend, and I think he was the greatest fighter of all times. And do you know what Joe used to do? He would study the pictures of his opponents over and over before a fight. And every professional man does the same thing.

"A doctor qualifies you by asking a lot of questions before he operates. He doesn't just say, 'Where's it hurt?' and then cut you open. That's the secret. I don't care if you're selling insurance, stocks, real estate, or for that matter anything at all. *You gotta qualify your customer!* The doctor says, 'Mr. Smith, according to all of the records I have, and all of the tests I ran, I think we got to remove your gall bladder. This is what I determine.' And the attorney does the same thing. He finds out all about the case before he can do anything for his client.

"Well, salesmen got to do the same thing. I seen too many salesmen who go right in, and they don't find out nothin' about the customer. They don't become his friend. They say, 'What d'ya wanna buy?' The customer says, 'I wanna buy a two-door Impala.' The salesman says, 'What d'ya want on it?' The customer says, 'A radio.' And the salesman shouts, 'Is that all?' Who the hell wants to buy from that kind of a salesman? He didn't ask the customer for his name. He didn't give him a card. He didn't even ask him to sit down! You have to treat the guy with some respect. You're going to ask him for $6,000. He's going to take home a payment book that's this thick." Joe gestures with his thumb and forefinger. "Why should he buy a car from that salesman? He's been with him for two minutes!"

Joe pauses, shakes his head. "Look at how some boys have so many girls and other guys don't have any. The guys who don't have them just aren't qualifying the girl. They're not sincere with her. They want to do things with the girl right away, but first they gotta sell themselves to the girl. After all, she has to like the guy before she'll even let him touch her, or whatever else. "Love is a game of selling." Joe grins. "You don't say to a girl after two minutes, 'C'mon, baby, let's go.' She'll slap your face. Just like a girl, the customer slapped the salesman's face! He walked away. I see it happen all the time. Then the salesman goes into the showroom with the other guys and tells them, 'Boy what a mooch that guy was. I gave him a good price and he didn't buy!' *Why should the guy buy from such a dummy? He was only with him for a minute and a half. He didn't even know the salesman's name. He didn't even give him a business card!*"

Just the thought of such selling upsets Joe. "In our business, you have to qualify the customer by asking him questions. Does he have a trade-in? Was the trade paid for? Has he shopped around and got any other prices from other dealers? Has he had a demonstration ride? These are all qualifying questions." Joe's voice rises emphatically, "*Getting to know you*.... That's the name of the game! Getting to know a little about the guy before you actually get into a sale!

"A guy will come in with high boots on with a lot of concrete or dirt on them. And a hard hat on." Joe acts out both descriptions. "I'll say, 'Mmm, you must be in the construction business.' Now, everybody likes to talk about himself. I try to open the guy up. The guy says, 'How did ya know?' I reply, 'Well, I saw the clothes, the boots. What're you in? Steel? Concrete?' You see, I'm interested in him, and I let him tell me about himself.

"Sometimes I'll just say, 'You know, I always try to find out, just by looking at a guy, what his profession is. No kiddin'. I bet you're a doctor.' The guy feels important. 'No, I'm not.' 'Well, what d'ya do?' 'You won't believe this, but I work at the Milstein Meat Company. They butcher cows.'

" 'You know, I've always wanted to see that, George. Say, can you get me in there so I can see it?' And I look at the guy like he's the most important person in the world to me. Well, the guy's interested in me 'cause I'm interested in him. He thinks that it's something great that he's doing. 'Do you mean to tell me that you actually slaughter these animals and it don't bother you?' 'Naw, Joe, ya get used to it.' 'Oh man, if I did that, it would bother me. Boy, I would like to see it. I really would. D'ya think you can get me in? . . . You can! When can I come?' ''

A big smile breaks over Joe's face. "I'll pick out a time of the day when there's not much action going on around the showroom, and I'll go visit the plant. He'll introduce me around and brag that I'm the guy he bought his car from. This gives me a chance to meet more people and sell more cars. And if another guy ever comes in who works for another meat company, I'll go through the same routine like this: 'Say, I once sold a car to a guy who works at Milstein Meat Company.' You see, I'm trying to relate to the customer. 'And he took me through the plant, and do you know that I couldn't sleep for two days. Boy, I'm telling you, that was really something else. Is it the same thing at your place?' 'Yeah, Joe, it's about the same thing.' 'You're killin' pigs though, aren't you?' 'Joe, we save everything with the pigs. Joe, we're even trying to figure out a way to save the squeal.' 'Boy, I would really like to see that. I really would . . . . How about if I come down to the plant between one and four on Thursday afternoon? . . . Say, that's just great!' ''

Joe schedules these visits strategically. "I want to get the hell out of the joint and prospect during the slow hours of the day. I once went to a place here in Detroit where they make gumballs. You should see the way they make gumballs. And I've been to a candy factory, a broaching factory, a screw machine shop. I said to the guy, 'What do you do all day?' He said, 'I screw all day. Actually, I make screws.' I said, 'No kiddin'. I just can't picture how they make screws. You know, I'd l-like to . . . say, c-could you get me in so I could see that? You would? Gee, that's great!' ''

Joe sits back in his chair and shouts, "You're getting the guy obligated and letting him see that he's important and that somebody cares for him. Probably nobody's ever asked him what he does. They say, 'You make screws—get screwed?'" Joe leans forward and lowers his voice. "But now the guy's thinking, Here's somebody who's really interested in me! I made him feel important. If you make a guy feel important, he'll take his wallet out and say, 'Here, take what you want.'"

Joe points to the telephone on his desk. "Another thing, I never take a telephone call when I'm with a customer. I tell the switchboard not to allow the phone to ring in my office and to take all calls. After all, an attorney don't answer the phone when he's pleading a case. And a doctor don't take phone calls when he's in the middle of surgery. Well, I'm just as important as they are, and I don't take calls neither! You know what will happen while you're taking a telephone call? The guy will cool off, that's what!"

As you look around Joe's office, you encounter no distractions. "How many times have you seen photos of different cars on a salesman's walls?" He chuckles. "Hell, that gets the customer confused! He'll start asking, 'How much is that one over there?' or 'Say, Joe, maybe I should look into that model.' There's nothing on my walls to confuse him or distract him. I don't have any of those color charts or undercoat choices up there to attract his attention. The only thing I got on my walls are my plaques. They let him know that he's dealing with *somebody*. And I'm somebody because I treated people good. That's how I became the Number One Car Salesman in the world."

Joe explains his office operations. "I got two employees who work for me. One of them is my son, Joey. They take the phone calls, do the demonstrations, fill out credit statements, and all the legwork, so's I can do only one thing: *Sell*. I only want to sell. That's what I do best, so that's the only thing I want to do. This way I'm not mentally tired . . . or bodily tired." Joe shrugs. "And, what the hell, in my tax bracket, what I pay them is being half paid by my partner, Uncle Sam. So, I always say that any top salesman worth his salt should have somebody else do the legwork."

Joe Girard knows how to put on a performance for his custom-

ers, and thousands of people who have bought cars or trucks from
him expect a show when they enter his office. And they know
that Joe really cares about them and their families, too.

"The first thing I do when a customer comes into my office is
give him a round button with an apple on it that says, 'I Like
You.' I give them to the wife and kids, too. And then I give the
kids these heart-shaped balloons that say, 'You'll Love a Joe
Girard Deal.' Y'know, people like people who are nice to their
kids. I get down on my hands and knees and say to the children,
'Hi. What's your name? Hi, Jimmy. Gee, you sure got a nice kid.
What a little cutie pie.' Then, while I'm still on my knees, I crawl
over to my cabinet with Jimmy, and his parents are watchin' all
the time! 'Jimmy, I got something for you. Wait till you see what
I got for you!' And I reach into my cabinet and pull out a fistful of
suckers. Then, while I'm still on my knees, I walk over to the
customer's wife and I say, 'Now, Jimmy, you take this one, and
here, Mama, you take the rest. And here are some balloons,
Daddy. Jimmy, Daddy will hold these for you. Now you be a
good boy while I'm talking to your mommy and daddy.' And all
this time, I'm on my knees. Well, these are gifts of obligation and
part of the tools of selling. Now, how could a guy say no to
somebody who's on his hands and knees with his kid?

"If a guy hits his pocket looking for cigarettes and says, 'I
thought I had some cigarettes,' I say, 'Just a minute,' and I go
into my cabinet and pull out about fifteen different brands. 'What
kind do you smoke?' He tells me, 'Pall Mall,' and I say, 'Oh,
here you are,' and I open it for him, I light a match, and I put the
pack right in his pocket. If he asks me, 'How much do I owe
you?' I'll say, 'Don't be silly.' What am I doing? *I'm obligating
him to me!* I buy the cigarettes wholesale. You know who pays
for it? Me and Uncle Sam!''

Joe pauses, then adds, "You know, I even have a bar in my
office. I've had many deals where the customer says, 'It sounds
like a good deal, Joe, but what I'd really like to do is go to a bar
and think it over.' I smile and say, 'Yeah, it takes a drink for me
too when it comes to a tough decision. What do you drink, Mr.

Brown?' And notice that I never say, 'Do you want a drink?' Well, whatever the guy drinks, you name it, and I pull it out of my cabinet.

"I always take out two bottles. His and mine. My bottle has colored water in it. That's rule number one. Never, ever, take a drink on the job. It gives you bad breath, and it slows down your thinking. It makes you stink. Who wants to deal with a lousy stinker! But you gotta drink with the guy. A lot of people are offended if you don't take a drink with them. 'Boy am I glad you brought it up, Mr. Brown. Boy I need a drink. Here's to your health and your family,' I toast, and I drink the colored water while he downs his drink. 'You'll be satisfied that you dealt with me, Mr. Brown. Go ahead and OK this form, will ya? Right here, Mr. Brown.' Now how's he gonna walk away from me after that drink? There's no way."

Joe treats the customer with care when he's selling, but he doesn't stop there. "One thing that I do that a lot of salesmen don't, and that's believe the sale really begins *after* the sale—not before! Most salesmen just figure, Now that I got ya, who needs ya. With me, I consider a sale a sacred thing. I consider you *my* customer and belonging to me, not to the dealership or General Motors. The customer is my private business. And I let him know it constantly.

"When he comes back for service, I fight for him all the way to get him the best. You won't believe the way I fight for him! I show people that I really care for them. And people see that and they appreciate it. They don't mind spending an extra twenty-five or thirty bucks, 'cause they know that I really care for them. When somebody calls me and says, 'I've been in twice, Joe, and nobody wanted to take care of me,' I say, 'That's your problem, 'cause do you remember me saying that if you ever have a problem, you should ask for me? Now why don't you come in around ten o'clock tomorrow and let me take care of it for you. I promise you that I will.'

"And when he does come in, I really go to bat for him. I find out who can help. If our service department can't do it, then I find out who can. Is it the factory man? Most salesmen won't bother to find out. If the factory man can't do it, then I go over his head. Who's his boss? And I tell him, 'Look, every time I talk to you, I'm told that it's the customer's fault. Now, I don't believe it. I'm gonna call Mr. White, and if Mr. White can't handle it, then I know who his boss is, too.' If I gotta, I'll go right up to Mr. Murphy, the chairman of the board of General Motors! Well, the guys say, 'Sure, you can do it 'cause your name is Joe Girard.' Well, at one time my name didn't mean a thing to those people. But I always made it a rule to find out who could help me if the service man couldn't. Or if the factory man couldn't help, then who could? If his boss couldn't help me, then I'd say, 'Who's your boss?' and I'd go to his boss. In other words, it's called *saving a customer!*

"You should see the way some of these salesmen treat their customers when they come back for service," Joe frowns. "Like I said, 'The sale begins *after* the sale,' and it don't make any difference what business you're in. If the customer was good enough to buy from you, then he deserves service. But, I've seen salesmen say, 'Oh no! Here comes that mooch again. He's always botherin' me. I can't get him off my back!' Now that's disgraceful. Here's a customer who spent $6,000 for a car, and in two years he's gonna buy another one. His wife drives, and so do his two sons. And the guys on the bowling team drive, and so do the people at the factory where he works. This guy can send some business to you. But these salesmen aren't willing to take two minutes to put him in the right hands. Hell, it only takes two stinkin' minutes. Yet they say, 'Go through that door, turn left, climb the ladder, swim over the roof, and ask for Mr. McFinnigan.' They're showing the guy that they don't like him!"

Joe's forehead wrinkles with concern. "You gotta be like a doctor, something's wrong with his car, so feel hurt for him. 'Gosh, I'm sorry to hear that.' 'Gee, that's a shame.' Then I turn to Nick, my right-hand man, and say, 'Nick, will you take Mr. Green over to service and make sure that he gets properly handled?' Well, it only took a couple of minutes, and the guy's saying to himself, 'I don't get it. This Girard's really sincere. He really cares!' The guy leaves, scratching his head, saying, 'I bought six cars and nobody ever cared. This Girard's a pretty nice guy' "

It's the attitude Joe has toward his customers that generates his sincerity. "Mr. Wilson, I want your business," pleads Joe with a hard-nosed customer. "Do you know what I want to do? I want you to give me the opportunity to prove that I'm going to give you the best service you ever had. And I know one thing, and that's that my deal's as good as, if not better than, anyone else's in town. And I want to be your salesman. So why don't you let me?" Then in a very low voice, "Just OK it there for me, will ya?" And Joe puts his pen on top of the order pad, so close to the customer that he can hardly resist.

"You know, some salesmen are afraid to ask for business. But not me. If I gotta, I'll literally get down on my knees and beg the guy for a sale. Hell, I'm not proud. 'Come on, give me a deal, will ya?' " Joe mimics on his knees. "Now how could ya say no to a forty-eight-year-old man who's on his knees. 'C'mon, give me a sale, will ya? What d'ya want me to do, lay on my back? OK, I'll lay on my back! What else? Give me a deal, will ya? Come on!' "

Joe gets up and continues. " 'Do you know what, Mr. Wilson? I hope you get a lemon. And I really mean this. I hope you get a lemon so's I can show off, because I will turn that lemon into a peach, and then I will own you for the rest of your life.' "

Joe's customers always walk away happy they decided to buy from him, because he does something that most salesmen never do. *He thanks them for their business and expresses his appreciation.* It's a simple gesture, but most salespeople just don't bother to let the customer know that they appreciate his business. " 'Mr. Wilson, I want you to know one thing. I'll never let you down. I really appreciate you buying from me. And believe me, by God, if you ever need me, if you ever see people around me, I will *drop* what I am doing *for you,* and I betcha you'll never buy a car from anybody else again. Because you're going to see that buying from me is going to be a thrill.'" Joe grins. "You know, I've heard people say, 'Buying a car is a hectic thing, and it actually scares me. You don't know who to believe. I've been told so many things, I don't trust any of those car salesmen. But, Joe, you've made buyin' a car a real thrill! You helped me, and you actually made it a privilege.' I've heard my customers say this so many times that I put it on my card, *Enjoy the thrill of a good deal*. And I don't put it on my card to burn up ink. I mean what I say."

Joe's sales don't stop when the customer leaves the showroom. "That customer ain't out the door, and my son has made up a thank-you note. It's just a simple note which tells him how much I appreciated his business. And look here," he says, pulling out one of his envelopes. "On the back of the envelope it says, 'I like you.' You see, I'm starting a relationship with him. All of my stationery has the same message on it. 'I like you.' It don't matter who I correspond with. If a guy wants a quote, the stationery says the same thing, 'I like you.' And I always enclose my business cards for him to pass out to his friends."

When the car is delivered, Joe always gives his customer a warm reception. "This is a proud moment in his life," Joe explains. "Show him that you're happy for him. Show him that you care for him. It don't matter what color the car is, the fact that he picked it out and General Motors makes it means that somebody must like it. 'My, what a beautiful car. Gee, don't it look good in that color!' I've seen some guys reply when the customer asks them for their opinion on a color, 'Well, what can I tell ya?' These salesmen are insulting his intelligence. It don't make a bit of difference what color it is, I'll always say, 'My, isn't it absolutely beautiful!' 'Say, Nick, isn't it a beauty?' 'You know, this is one of the hottest colors. It's just gorgeous!'

"It's these same salesmen," Joe comments with disgust, "who toss the keys to the customer and say, 'It's parked outside on the side of the building,' when the car is delivered. I believe that if you show the customer that you really care for him, he'll show you that he'll bring in more business for you, because you're doing something that nobody else ever did for him. And it makes a lot of sense. Nobody wants to be treated like a schlemiel.''

While delivering the car, Joe takes out a stack of twenty-five or so business cards and sticks them in the glove compartment, announcing, "Wherever you go, Mr. Green, I go. And remember what I told you. Every time you send me a customer, there's twenty-five bucks in it for you. Now don't forget to tell your friends how good I treated you. Just make sure that your name's on the back of the card, and tell 'em to get a couple of prices before they come to me. Now don't forget . . . ."

Joe boasts with a grin, "I've got the biggest bird-dog system in the world. As soon as I get through with a sale, I give them a stack of cards, and I'm automatically hiring them to work for me. I tell them to say, 'Just go and see my friend, Joe. He'll take real good care of you.' ''*

With all the sincerity Joe Girard radiates when he's selling an automobile, he has one uncommon sales technique. "I never look a customer in the eyes when I'm asking him for a deal," he confesses. "Sure, I know that we've all been brainwashed to look a person squarely in the eye, 'cause that's supposed to mean you're honest, but the guy can *feel* it when I'm selling him. Hell, it's in my voice. So when I tell him, 'Put your OK right here,' or 'Give me a hundred and fifty bucks,' I'm always looking somewhere else. I don't want to see his head shaking that he don't wanna buy. If he hesitates, sometimes I'll break the tension with a line like 'What'sa matter, you got arthritis or something? Come on, will ya? Give me some money. You only got a hundred twenty-five? That's all right. Give me a hundred and keep the twenty-five bucks for yourself.' The point is, I'm mever looking him in the eye, because if he's hesitating, I don't want to see it!

"Another thing, if a guy don't have any money to give me, I say, 'That's all right. I'll take your word for it. It's good enough

*The practice of payment for referral sales is prohibited in several states.

for me.' I mean, what's the use of arguing with him like I've seen other salesmen do? If he comes through with the money, then that's great. If he don't, then he don't.'' Joe shrugs.

"Speaking of closing a sale," Joe continues, "people always ask me, 'How d'ya close?' I simply close by treating people nice. Treating people like they're important. That's it! Treating people like I'm the guy who you should buy from. *'You won't be sorry* if you buy from me!' ''

Joe's customers won't forget him once they buy a car from him; he won't let them! Every month throughout the year, they get a letter from him. It arrives in a plain envelope, always a different size or color. "It doesn't look like that junk mail which is thrown out before it's even opened," Joe confides. "And they open it up, and the front of it reads, 'I LIKE YOU.' Inside it says, 'Happy New Year, from Joe Girard.' '' He sends a card in February wishing customers a "Happy George Washington's Day." In March, it's "Happy St. Patrick's Day.''

"I can just see the kids and wife standing around when the husband comes home," Joe marvels. "The first thing he does is kiss his wife, and then he asks two questions. First, 'How were the kids today?' And second, 'Did I get any mail?' Soon the kids are shouting, 'Yeah, Daddy, you got somethin' from Joe Girard.' The whole family gets in on the act. They love those cards. You should hear all the comments I get on them. D'ya know that I send out over 13,000 cards every month? And everyone of them says, 'I like you . . . Have a Happy Fourth of July,' or 'I like you . . . Happy Thanksgiving.' There's nothin' else on the card. Nothin' but my name. I'm just telling 'em that I like 'em.''

Joe Girard obviously does a good job selling himself to his customers. They remember him; in 1976, an astonishing *65 percent* of his sales were repeat sales. That, too, is a world record! What his customers are saying is "We like you, too, Joe Girard.''

2

Joe M. Gandolfo

(LIFE INSURANCE)

"Selling is 98 percent understanding human beings . . . 2 percent product knowledge."

Joe Gandolfo sells more life insurance each year than any other person in the world. His production exceeds $800 million each year, and in 1975 he sold an amount of life insurance in excess of *$1 billion!*

He holds the CLU designation as a member of the American College of Life Underwriters. He is past president of the Lakeland Association of Life Underwriters; past vice president of the Polk County, Florida, Estate Planning Board; and past member of the editorial board of *Leaders Magazine.* Twice he has received the National Sales Masters Award. Joe is also a member of the Lakeland Chamber of Commerce, the Saul Heubner Foundation, and the Golden Key Society. He is a life and qualifying member of the Million Dollar Round Table, a member of the board of directors of the Church of the Resurrection, and a member of the American College of Life Underwriters Development Fund.

Joe is the author of three books: *Ideas Are a Dime a Dozen, On to a Hundred Million,* and *Selling Is 98% Understanding Human Beings . . . 2% Product Knowledge.* His recordings "How to Earn $100,000 a Year As a Salesman" and "$40,000,000 of Life Insurance in Two Years" have been translated into several languages. He has given speeches in every state in the union and in Canada, Mexico, and some European countries, averaging about fifty speeches per year.

He serves as a consultant to American National Life Insurance Company, and has in past years advised several other insurance companies. Presently he is an automobile industry consultant and claims to have more than 4,200 dealers as clients.

In 1971, Joe was selected as one of the Outstanding Young Men in America by the Junior Chamber of Commerce.

Joe was born on March 13, 1936, in Richmond, Kentucky. He attended Kentucky Military Institute, Vanderbilt University, Miami University of Ohio, and the Wharton School of Finance. After playing professional minor-league baseball for one year in 1958, he was a high school teacher and athletic coach in Fort Lauderdale, Florida. In 1960, he joined the Kennesaw Life Insurance Company, beginning his training at Baton Rouge, Louisiana.

With his wife, Carol, and their children, Mike, Diane, and Donna, Joe lives in Lakeland, Florida, where he operates as an independent insurance agent representing forty-five life insurance companies.

He and his family are tennis enthusiasts. Mike, Diane, and Donna are All-Americans, and Joe is the national chairman of the Men's 35 and Over. For five years he sponsored the Gandolfo Invitational Men's 35 Event at Forest Hills, New York.

Joe Gandolfo makes selling seem so simple. He claims that you only have to understand people and you too can sell several hundred million dollars' worth of life insurance each year. Wow, you might think, Gandolfo really understood a lot of people in 1975 when he sold more than *one billion dollars*. He probably understands people better than any man on earth.

Well, perhaps he does. Especially when it comes to selling them life insurance. After all, people in the insurance industry get excited about anyone who sells a million dollars of life insurance in a year. But even a million-dollar-a-year salesman would have to sell for a thousand years to equal Gandolfo's production figures for 1975 alone.

Gandolfo's selling is like running a mile in less than two minutes, or like a major-league baseball player hitting a hundred home runs in a single season. Sure, doubting Thomases protest, "That's absurd. It simply can't be done."

In fact, Joe is often asked, "Did you *really* write over a billion in a single year? Tell me, Joe, aren't you stretching it just a little bit when you say *a billion?*"

"When I hear comments like that," Joe replies in his soft Southern accent, "I just tell them that the only thing that needs stretching is their minds."

JOE M. GANDOLFO

Joe makes such statements often but doesn't offend his listeners, because he speaks with complete sincerity. It is this sincerity which probably generates the super self-confidence that is evident when you're around him. It doesn't matter whether you're talking to him on the phone or sitting across a desk from him, you can feel the vibrations in the air. Where does it all start? Well, according to Joe, it begins with a salesman believing in his product.

"I think that you can't do whatever it is that you do effectively," Joe claims, "unless you believe in it 100 percent. I believe in life insurance. Do you know what? Before I owned a million on my own life, I couldn't sell a million, because I didn't see how anyone could afford it. Then, when I owned a million and several million after that, it became easy for me to talk with a great deal of conviction about why my prospect needed a million or several million.

"The same thing applies to tax shelters. Once I began to put my own money into tax shelters, I discovered that it became a lot easier for me to convince the other guy to put his money into them. People at my income level are always asking me, 'Say, Joe, are you in it?' and I can proudly say, 'Yeah.'"

This "Yeah" is a powerful answer. Joe says it with conviction, conveying to his client "Look, if I have it, then you know what I think of it."

In fact, Joe believes in his product so much that he *knows* that every person he has an appointment with is going to buy from him. Most salesmen begin to assume the sale is made when the prospect starts nodding his head, asking questions about the premium, or wanting to know if he'll have to take an examination. Those are the normal buying signals, and Joe admits that he used to look for such things when he began his career in the life insurance business. "The only buying signal I need now is an appointment." Joe grins. "When he consents to have me come out to see him, that's it! I know he's interested in talking about life insurance, so he evidently has a need to buy some. After all, he's not consenting to see me for his health, is he?"

Isn't it completely logical that the world's number one life insurance agent is going to sell to a prospect, since anyone who agrees to see him needs to buy life insurance? *Gandolfo thinks so!* Yet, the majority of insurance salespeople approach each appointment with fear that they're not going to make a sale! Perhaps it's a conditioned reflex they've developed because they're accustomed to failing. How it it, then, that a man like Joe Gandolfo can be so positive about succeeding?

Joe believes that success begins with faith. A Roman Catholic, he goes to Mass each day of his life. "I don't care if you are Jewish, Mormon, Protestant, or Catholic, it doesn't make any difference. Every giant that I have met believes in this number one fundamental."

Joe shrugs. "I'm no saint, far from it. I have the same temptations that any other person has, but I put things in their proper perspective. He comes first and I never let Him forget it. The mark of a great athlete is the ability to concentrate. You can't concentrate on something if you are not right with the Man Upstairs. I can be looking at you and telling you the truth, but if I'm not right with Him, I won't come across as telling you the truth."

Joe's rapid speech suddenly stops. He says in a whisper, "You know, I don't understand why this is so, and I'm not too sure if I am supposed to. But, I'll tell you this much, people write to me or call me, and they complain that they're having trouble selling life insurance. I immediately ask then what their religion is. After they tell me, I ask them if they practice it. Well, so often they tell me that they don't have time!"

Joe sighs. "I don't understand that. When you're talking to a prospect about his life insurance and thinking about dying, how can you concentrate on the client and his problem when something else is cluttering your mind? When you don't close, perhaps you think that it is something technical. You blame the policy, the net cost, or maybe you say it's your manager's fault. No, those aren't the reasons you're not selling. The first thing you have to do is be right with the Man Upstairs in your own way.

"Each morning when I leave home, the Good Man Upstairs and I have a conversation. I tell him, 'Lord, I'll give you all the credit, I'll take all the commissions.' A warm smile appears on Joe's face. "You know, it's been working pretty well."

Of course, Joe doesn't rely on prayers alone to get results. He's up at five every morning. During the early years of his career, he worked seven days a week.

"I had a young man come to see me recently," he recalls, "who wanted to know how he could double his production of two and a half million. Well, I asked him to tell me something about his typical day. He replied, 'I get up about six-thirty or seven in the morning, have breakfast with my wife and the kids, then I take the kids to school and get to the office about a quarter to nine.'

" 'We don't need to talk anymore,' I said. 'Why?' he wanted to know. I told him that he was wasting half his life. I explained that he doesn't sell his wife and his kids at breakfast and he won't get paid to take them to school. But if that's what he wanted to do, well, then, I thought he was happy doing just that. But I told him not to come to me and say he would like to double his production. I went on to explain to him that it takes sacrifice, and unfortunately, it is sacrificing your family.

"There's one thing you've got to understand about successful people," Joe emphasizes. "Successful people usually are the ones who get up early to go to work. And because they do, they respect a salesman who's willing to do the same thing. When an insurance agent asks to see a businessman during his work day and he gets turned down, the prospect is really saying, 'Look here, Mr. Insurance Man, you work from nine to five and that's when I work, from nine to five. I'm making money then and I don't want to take time away from making money to talk about dying or to help you make money.'

" 'Can I see you at six-thirty or seven-thirty in the morning?' I ask. I'm really saying, 'When you're not busy making money, I would like to talk to you about your problems so that you can concentrate on what I'm saying. I'm on call twenty-four hours a day. When are you not making money? When is that time? We can talk then.' I guarantee that with the majority of successful people, that time is six-thirty, seven-thirty, or eight in the morning; noon; or five, six, or seven at night. Sometimes I'll have three breakfasts or three lunches." Joe chuckles.

Joe knows that successful people respect his willingness to meet with them in the early morning, and he claims that the majority of his sales have been made before nine A.M. "The successful people I know," Joe asserts, "say to themselves, 'This Gandolfo works as hard at his job as I do at mine; therefore, he must be as astute in his field as I am in mine.' You see, all of the people I work with, well, none of them inherited their fortune. They all worked very hard for it. They can identify with hard work, and they don't like loafers.

"It's with this in mind that I quickly identify myself as a hard worker when I first speak with a prospect," Joe explains. "I tell him that I'm considered in many circles to be the number one life insurance agent in the United States. I've been written up in the *Wall Street Journal, Fortune, Forbes,* and several other magazines. Then I put my business card down and say, 'John, there are about 400,000 life insurance agents and financial counselors on the face of this earth, and I think it's important that you know about my qualifications for coming here in the first place. If you'll permit me, I'd like to tell you something about myself.

" 'In the upper left-hand corner of the card you'll find *Million Dollar Round Table,* in the upper right-hand corner, the initials *NQA.* These two are industry awards. There are only 13,000 to 14,000 members of the Million Dollar Round Table, and there are only 4,000 to 5,000 Life and Qualifying members. NQA means that over 90 percent of all men and women with whom I have done business have *continued* doing business with me. I'll either call you on the phone or see you in person once a year to review your program. I'm interested in a long and enduring relationship. The CLU after my name stands for Chartered Life Underwriter, synonymous to CPA in the accounting field. I give numerous talks throughout the United States on life insurance. I'm a member of St. Joseph Catholic Church.'

"Early in my career, I would tell a prospect that I was on

schedule for the Million Dollar Round Table, that I was on schedule to become a CLU, that I was a member of the National Association of Life Underwriters, and that I belonged to my company's President's Club.

"What am I doing? I'm letting him know that there's a good reason why he should do business with me. And it's a reason he can identify with. *Hard work!* He respects hard work.

"Of course, now my reputation works for me," Joe explains. "Many of my clients will introduce me as the number one life insurance man in the world. In fact, they like to brag about it. They take pride in knowing that I'm their agent."

The walls of Joe's office are adorned with dozens of awards and honors that he has received over the years. He freely admits that they are displayed in order to let his client know about his achievements. "Sometimes I'll even excuse myself for a few minutes so he can take a look around the room and get a good look at them," Joe confesses. "What the hell, I'm proud of the recognition that I've received. After all, there's a good reason why I'm number one. I want him to know that I worked hard for my awards."

Joe also has many of his favorite quotations on the office walls. One reads, "Everybody wants to go to heaven, but nobody wants to die." This reflects his philosophy about paying a price for success. He respects hard work, and he knows that other successful people share this respect.

After the client knows about Joe, they have a lengthy session together. Joe often spends a full day with a big client, and the warm-up session may go on for several hours while Joe asks hundreds of questions. "A lot of agents spend a great deal of their time doing research prior to an actual interview. I do none," explains Joe. "I don't want to know anything, because if you go in with preconceived notions, then you have already formed an opinion. That's wrong. How would you like to go to your doctor and have him say, 'Oh, here comes Bob Brown. I think I'll give him this prescription.'

"So I begin by asking him all kinds of questions. A typical set of questions might be 'Where were you born? What did your parents do? Are they still living? Do you have any brothers and sisters? Tell me about them. What's your education? Where did you go to school? How did you get into the automobile business? Tell me how you got to where you are today.' And I continue to ask him questions with only a legal-size pad and a pen in front of me.

"As we progress, I ask more complicated questions, such as 'Do you have any insurance on your wife? What's your philosophy about insurance for your wife? How about the children? Do they have any insurance? How do you expect to educate them? Do you have a buy-sell agreement? Is it funded with life insurance? What are your thoughts on this? Do you have a stock redemption agreement? Is it funded with life insurance? Are you in a pension or a profit-sharing plan? I see that you just bought this building for a million dollars; do you have any mortgage insurance? Do you think it is important? You just bought this company for $98 million. Do you have any key-man insurance? Does it really make any difference whether the guy is there or not?

" 'What financial formula did you use to arrive at the present amount of life insurance that you now have?' And I continue to find out as much information as I can about him.'' As Joe speaks, he points to another statement on his office wall. It reads, ''God gave you two ears and one mouth, and He meant for you to do twice as must listening as talking.''

Joe's warm-up session is what he considers the embodiment of his philosophy that ''selling is 98 percent understanding human beings and 2 percent product knowledge.'' ''You'll never really understand people unless you go out and meet them.'' Joe raises his soft voice as he stresses, ''Asking a lot of questions and doing a lot of listening, well, that's the best way to understand people. Because if you do all the talking, how can you understand 'em? You'd never get to know anyone if you did all the talking. And another thing: I'm genuinely interested in this guy. I really want to know how he got into business, and I want to know all about his philosophies. I want to find out everything I can about him, because I think he's an interesting person. And, I'll tell you something else. I come away a better person because I learned a lot from this man.

"You see, I really love these people. It's a genuine trait of mine." Again, Joe's sincerity comes through, blending with his self-confidence.

Joe believes that most salesmen's biggest problem is that they do too much talking in their sales interviews. "By asking a lot of questions and then shutting up and listening, I find that I sell more insurance," Joe states. "Prospects will end up selling themselves. In fact, I believe that a good rule for a salesman to follow is to count up to five after the prospect has finished speaking before you say anything. Too many salesmen bombard the client with conversation just because he pauses for a moment. That will often break his train of thought and possibly offend him. You have to remember that a man's voice is one of the greatest sounds in the world to him, so let him talk when he wants to. There's no way you can be genuinely interested in him if you don't listen to what he's saying.

"Another thing, when you're talking to a client, always look him in the eye, and never take your eyes away. When you're listening, look at his mouth, and nod your head slowly, and never take your eyes off of him. I'll guarantee you that doing that will do more for selling than any of the technical information that you learn from a rate book or attending a school.

"What do you think your client's going to think if you're looking at his good-looking wife or daughter when you're in his home? Or if you're having breakfast with a client and you're staring at a good-looking girl across the room? Your eyes are telling him that you're more interested in looking at her than you are in talking to him. You're signaling to him that he's not very important; *that's* what you're telling him."

Another important factor in Joe's success stems from his philosophy of specialization. During the past few years, Joe has specialized in selling to automobile dealers. In fact, throughout his career he has used a similar technique.

"When I first started in the life insurance business," Joe recalls, "I would always approach a client with the idea that I was an expert in his or her field. My approach to a man I have never met would be 'My name is Joe Gandolfo, and I'm with the Kennesaw Life Insurance Company. I didn't drop by today to discuss any life insurance, but came to ask for an opportunity to meet with you sometime next week to share an idea with you that has been of help to other pharmacists [schoolteachers, farmers, contractors, etc.] here in Lakeland. Would next Tuesday at two o'clock be convenient, or would three be better?'

"When I tell him that I would like to share an idea that has been of help to other people in his occupational group, it accomplishes two things. First, it implies that I am a specialist in matters concerning his group. Second, he's going to feel like an oddball if he's not willing to discuss ideas which apply to his occupation. Well, right off the bat it sets me up as *an expert*. Immediately I'm a specialist in his own particular vocation, and it seems that, for some reason or another, everyone thinks that his or her problems are different from other people's, and that is exactly what I capitalize on.

"Most recently I've been specializing in calling on automobile dealers. I think that the key to finding a particular group is to find one that you really feel comfortable with and that you can identify with. Then you just go from there. I can identify with automobile dealers because my dad was one. They have some fine qualities too. For example, they're able to make decisions quickly. They've got a lot of money. They're hard workers, and most of them are self-made men. I guess most important is the fact that *they need me*. They don't have anyone who can talk their language or get tough when you gotta get tough. And they need estate planning and tax shelters because they're building an empire and they don't have time to conserve it. And 99 percent of the dealers I call on don't have wills or trusts, nor have they done any estate planning.

"Of course," Joe continues, "I dare say that you would find this to be true if you worked with any other field. Farmers, doctors, implement dealers . . . I just happened to pick this field. But it's going to apply to contractors, citrus people—hell, they're all in the same boat crying for somebody to help them. I just happen to love automobile dealers because they're good people. They're honest, lovable people, that's all. They have a great passion for their employees, and they really appreciate someone like myself who won't waste their time and knows what he's talking about.''

Joe's reputation among automobile dealers has spread throughout the country, and he now spends much of his time consulting with them as well as selling them insurance. It's not uncommon, for example, for him to be referred by a Chicago Oldsmobile dealer to an Oldsmobile dealer in Detroit. "Sure, perhaps there's some truth about the adage 'The expert is the guy from the next town,' " Joe admits, "but more important, I think many business people don't care to have the local guys know everything about them.''

Joe has always believed that it's very important for a life insurance agent to create the right image. "For example," he explains, "when I set up an appointment for an interview, I'll say, 'Can I see you at two-thirty on Wednesday, or would four on Friday be more convenient?' Well, he's going to be thinking, Gee, this Gandolfo must really have a tight schedule! Also, notice that I give him a choice of times, not a yes-or-no-type question, on whether or not he'll consent to the interview.

"Another thing I did in the early days of my career," Joe continues, "was to create an image of *always being busy.* If someone didn't show up for an appointment, after waiting several minutes for the guy I would either find a quiet spot in the park to read or perhaps I'd visit the library. I would never go to a place such as a restaurant where people could see me. I didn't want them to be thinking, This guy must not be busy if he has so much time to be sitting around drinking coffee and socializing all day. Naturally, I would try to use this time to be productive, but more important, I would avoid creating the appearance of having nothing to do.''

Joe grins. "Of course, now I don't have to appear to be busy. Hell, I'm so busy nowadays that I don't even have time to eat or sleep!"

It's interesting to note that on the day of Joe's interview with this author, he claims to have had seventeen people call him for appointments to discuss purchasing life insurance and tax shelters. "I can't see 'em until sometime next year." Joe shrugs.

Joe believes that the demand for his services is due to the fact that he sells *concepts* instead of a specific product. "When I call a client nowadays, I say, 'My name is Joe Gandolfo. I'm in the insurance and tax shelter business, and I'm assuming that you pay more than $4,000 a year in taxes, personal or corporate, and I'd like to run some ideas by you. If they fit with your philosophy and pocketbook, fine; if not, I promise you I'll be on my way. Would you have any objections to that?'

"The same approach is used when I call on my automobile dealer clients. I simply say, 'I would like to share ideas with you that have been of help to other automobile dealers. I just want to run them by you.' Now this same two-step approach would work on doctors, accountants, farmers, or anyone else. Part one is philsophy; if he likes it, fine. Part two is: Can he afford it? That's why I say 'if it fits in with your *philosophy* and *pocketbook*.'

"Even when I get an objection, such as 'Look, Joe, I have enough insurance,' I then say, 'Before I leave, may I ask you a question?' Well, this puts him at ease. He thinks I'm gonna ask him a question and then get the hell outa there.

" 'Mr. Prospect, you may recall from when you studied history in high school or college that during President Adams' administration Congress came within three votes of abolishing the Patent Office. The reason was that they wanted to save the taxpayer money. They thought that everything had been conceived. Since then we have had rockets to the moon, color television, electronic equipment, and who knows what all.'

" 'What's the point?' he'll say.

" 'The point is, have you closed your patent office?'

" 'Mr. Car Dealer, you probably think that this is pretty corny, but let's get right down on our level. If we opened a drugstore, wouldn't we stock our shelves with the latest drugs so that we could sell them?

"'You go to seminars and attend meetings to upgrade your level of knowledge. We have new ideas and concepts, and tax laws change every year. All I want to do is run them by you. If they fit in with your philosophy and pocketbook, fine; if not, I promise you I'll be on my way. Certainly you couldn't have any objections to that, could you?'"

Joe sits back in his chair, then adds, "An industrial psychologist for Ford Motor Company told me that many Fords are sold because of the ad with one microphone on the outside of the car and another one on the inside. You roll up the windows, and the ride is quieter on the inside than it is on the outside. The ad sells a quieter ride, but, to the best of my knowledge, it's always going to be quieter when you roll up the windows. Again, they're selling a concept.

"I can remember when a guy once told me that he bought insurance from a particular agent because he was told that if he became disabled, that particular company would pay the premiums on his policy for him. Hell, this agent was smart. He didn't tell him that 1,854 other companies will do the same thing with a waiver of premium rider. He simply told him, '*We'll* pay the premiums.' Again, an idea was sold.

"I can remember buying a television set because of an idea. I didn't want to get off the couch. I wanted to click it off and on.

"My idea is 'Are you paying more than $4,000 in taxes, personal or corporate?' Automobile dealers hate to pay the Internal Revenue Service, just like everyone else hates to."

After pausing to catch his breath, Joe adds, "Another thing I want to emphasize is that in my telephone interview I always say, 'Mr. Auto Dealer, I want you to be sure to include at our meeting any persons you believe are necessary so that you can make a decision when I see you next month. If you can't make a decision without your CPA, then have him there. If you need your attorney, or your controller, fine. If necessary, have them all present.'

You see, this sets the stage so he can't procrastinate when it comes time to make a decision during the interview.

"Also, I always attempt to give a presentation in such a manner so I don't confuse anyone. Of course, sometimes this is difficult to do when you're discussing a sophisticated subject such as tax shelters. And if there's a group of people in the room, usually there's one of them who is the decision maker, so I observe everyone very carefully so I can determine who should be the person I direct most of my attention to. Sometimes it's the CPA or perhaps the guy's attorney. It may be the one doing all the talking, or it can be the quiet guy who doesn't say anything, but everyone always turns to him so that they can see his reaction. It's difficult to explain. I suppose I just developed this horse sense which comes from experience."

The novice salesman may become confused and ask, "Isn't Gandolfo's philosophy about selling being 98 percent understanding human beings and only 2 percent product knowledge a little off base? Come on now. He's a CLU, and those tax shelter and pension plans take a hell of a lot of knowledge."

Gandolfo has heard this objection, and he acknowledges, "Sure, you have to know what you're talking about. In fact, even now I spend a few hours every day studying, you know, reading to keep up on the latest that's happening in the pension and taxation field. So please understand me when I say that I'm not underestimating the importance of knowledge.

"But I still maintain that it's not product knowledge but the *understanding of human beings* that makes a salesman effective. Hell, there's thousands of professors who have all kinds of knowledge, but they'd starve to death if they attempted to sell for a living. And there's all these brilliant guys behind their little desks at insurance companies' home offices who're experts on the product. So while the product knowledge is important, it takes something else to be an effective salesman." Joe leans back in his chair and says, "It's like I said, 'Selling is 98 percent understanding human beings and 2 percent product knowledge.'"

3

Bernice H. Hansen

(AMWAY)

"Being a positive thinker..."

Bernice Hansen is a Crown Direct Distributor of products manufactured and sold by Amway Corporation. She and her late husband, Fred, were among the first distributors to represent Amway
when it was founded in 1959. Bernice and Fred Hansen were in
fact in on the ground floor of a business that today is among the
largest direct sales organizations in the world. Amway has more
than 250,000 distributorships, which for fiscal 1976 generated
revenue in excess of $240 million.

In 1968, Fred Hansen died, leaving a giant-sized sales organization that included more than 60,000 Amway distributorships.
Bernice, who had been working side by side with her husband
until his untimely death, then assumed full responsibility for operating the family business. Today, the Hansen family business
involves more than 130,000 Amway distributorships.

In 1974, when Bernice Hansen was interviewed by the
Washington *Post,* she was asked how much money she earned
per year. She refused to say. The *Post* cited her age at the time as
eighty-three, when in fact she was sixty-three. Bernice says, "If
they misquoted my age by such a difference, just imagine what
they would have done had I told them my annual income!" Al-

though her income won't be specified here either, Bernice does indeed receive a sizable one.

Bernice has won virtually every honor awarded by Amway. She is a member of the board of directors of the Amway Distributors Association of the U.S., and in 1969 she founded the Executive Women's Council, which has chapters throughout the United States and Canada. One of the highlights of her career occurred in 1975, when she addressed the largest-ever Amway convention audience of more than 30,000 distributors in the huge Capitol Center Arena in Washington, D.C. She is often referred to as the "First Lady of Amway."

Bernice (née Hancock) was born on August 1, 1911, in Muskegon, Michigan. Her previous business experience was in accounting, and for three years prior to entering the sales field she and her husband operated a house trailer business in Akron, Ohio.

She has three daughters: Mary Anne Walker; Karen Hussey, who is an area coordinator for Amway at the company's home office in Ada, Michigan (Karen's husband, Jim, is regional sales manager at Amway); and Suzan Ross, whose husband, Skip, was an Amway distributor in California. In 1971, the Hansen and Ross sales organizations merged into a partnership, which is headquartered in Akron, Ohio. Bernice herself recently relocated to Grand Rapids, Michigan.

While there are more than 250,000 distributorships representing Amway, Bernice Hansen is one of only nine who have been recognized by achieving a "Crown." Amway Corporation's distributors sponsor other distributors. It is a unique company with a phenomenal growth record. It would take too long to explain the company's complicated sales structure in this chapter; the sole purpose of mentioning the sponsoring program is to inform the reader that Bernice Hansen's "Amway family" consists of an estimated 130,000 distributorships that she directly or indirectly sponsored.

"Of course," Bernice is quick to mention, "I get as little as one tenth of one percent from most of the sales. But," she adds, smiling, "even one tenth of one percent can add up. Last year, we had a $24 million increase.

"This is the most wonderful business in the world," Bernice enthuses. "We're just one big happy family at Amway. We're the most highly motivated, positive-thinking, goal-oriented group of people on the surface of this earth."

When Bernice Hansen makes such a statement, nobody who is familiar with Amway can deny that what she says is correct; but if you know Bernice you'll recognize that she is also describing herself. She is a living reflection of the company whose products she markets and has come to love so dearly. Amway is a thoroughly integral part of Bernice's life, and in order to understand her story fully, one must know the Amway story.

Richard DeVos and Jay Van Andel founded Amway in 1959 in the basements of their homes in Grand Rapids, Michigan. With more than $240 million in revenue during fiscal 1976, the company has become one of America's fastest-growing and most exciting enterprises. The company's product line consists mainly of everyday commodities, such as soaps, detergents, and personal-care items. In recent years, Amway has expanded its line to over 150 products, including thousands of individual items, ranging from agricultural products and smoke detectors to a weight-control program. The laundry compound is still its best seller.

Amway's basic sales philosophy has always been to market products such as toothpaste that everybody uses and that are not only easy to sell but will be reordered again and again. Most important, the products require no specialized training to sell, nor do they take technical expertise to demonstrate. Everyone, for example, knows how to use a bar of soap. "Why do we sell soap?" DeVos asks in one of his speeches. "Because people *buy* soap!"

Amway products don't require the salesperson to create demand, because there's no question that the customer needs them. They don't have installation or maintenance problems. The products are priced very competitively, and the Amway distributor offers personal service by bringing them to the customer's home. What's more, if the customer isn't satisfied, Amway has an unconditional money-back guarantee.

While many corporations offer quality products like those sold by Amway, there are certain dynamic personal characteristics that co-founders Van Andel and DeVos possess and which they have passed along to their associates. Their philosophies and principles played an important role in the spectacular Amway success story.

BERNICE H. HANSEN

"When my husband, Fred, and I first met Jay and Rich," Bernice recalls, "they were only twenty-three and twenty-four years old. Although Fred was forty-two at the time, he immediately recognized the excellent leadership of these fine young men.

"To give you some background, Fred was a barber for nine years in Grand Rapids. After many customers told him about the great opportunities that existed in sales, we decided in 1946 to close up the shop, and we moved to Akron, Ohio, where we went into the house trailer business with a cousin.

"But we didn't like that kind of selling, and in those days there was a serious problem in obtaining the retail financing for a house trailer. By chance in 1950, when we were back in Grand Rapids to get some retail financing, on my way out of a restaurant I happened to bump into Walter Bass, an old friend of Fred's. Well, Walt began to tell me about the wonderful business he was in and to ask about Fred. We respected Walt's opinion because he had sold radio advertising for twenty-five years and had many contacts with businessmen, so we figured he would be a good judge of business opportunities.

"Walt introduced us to Jay and Rich, who were then selling a food supplement called 'Nutrilite' that cost $19.50 for a one-month supply. At that time the entire sales force consisted of ten to twelve persons, including a barber, three milkmen, a druggist, and some housewives. After meeting with them, Fred and I went back to Akron and started our new business. I often think about those early days in Rich's basement, and all the coffee we drank during sales meetings.

"And I can remember Rich and Jay giving us a plan to make twenty contacts a day for ninety days. We were told that if we were willing to work the plan that they laid out to us on a day-to-day basis, we would develop a nucleus of retail customers, and from that nucleus we would build our sales organization," Bernice continues. "We recognized their fine leadership immediately because they gave us the exact plan which they themselves were working and succeeding with. When we had five couples assembled in our home, Rich and Walt Bass drove 325 miles in an old Packard from Grand Rapids to Akron to conduct a sales meeting. All five couples joined us.''

The Hansen couple were eager to succeed, and they adopted the principles of the hardworking young men who believed in leading by example. In 1959, Van Andel and DeVos founded Amway Corporation and began marketing many household products instead of exclusively selling Nutrilite products. The small family-type business grew rapidly after those early years and today Amway has far outgrown the basements of the DeVos and the Van Andel homes. Its headquarters in Ada, Michigan, cover over a million square feet on a three-hundred-acre site.

"But we maintain that family atmosphere,'' Bernice insists. "No matter how large Amway becomes, we still place a strong emphasis on closeness. In fact, we're structured so that when a distributor gets to be a certain size, he or she becomes a direct distributor and maintains a new sales organization which deals directly with Amway. The whole system is geared to provide an incentive for everyone to grow and be justly compensated; however, the individual never loses his or her identity.''

As Bernice tells the Amway story, one senses her affection for the company. "We're like a bunch of kissin' cousins.'' She laughs. "Recently we had a convention at the Breakers in West Palm Beach, Florida, for our Diamond distributors. There must have been about fifty to sixty distributorships down there, and as they began pouring in at the registration desk, everybody was greeting everybody else with hugging and kissin'. Well, this one old-timer who was a guest at the hotel turned to his wife and I heard him say, 'Boy, it looks like we've got a real wild, swinging group this weekend!'

"We have several get-togethers during the year with other distributors,'' Bernice continues, "and over the years we've all become very close friends. Between the wonderful vacations we've had in such places as Hawaii, the Caribbean, and Europe, and our sales conventions, we're just one big happy family. It's a wonderful experience to be a part of such a group. And even with our present size, Jay and Rich have worked very hard to keep that 'family touch' like we had in the beginning. Of course, today is different from when we had just a handful of people around the kitchen table conducting a sales meeting while drinking coffee. But, nevertheless, we've maintained a definite family atmosphere within the Amway organization, and this atmosphere doesn't exist in other companies.''

Bernice pauses for a moment, then explains, "It's very important to note that the vast majority of our distributorships are run by husband-and-wife teams. So we place a great deal of emphasis on the family. Of course, Jay and Rich are devoted family men, so they realize its strong positive influence on a salesperson. Additionally, our products are of a household and personal-care nature, so again, everything is geared for the family.''

In 1968, when he was fifty-nine, Fred Hansen suffered a heart attack just three weeks after taking a physical examination for a $100,000 life insurance policy that was never issued. He died five and a half weeks later. During his last weeks in an intensive care unit, Bernice recalls how contented Fred felt because he knew that his wife and three daughters would be provided for with an ongoing business that would ensure their prosperity.

Although Bernice had neither run a sales seminar nor done recruiting before Fred's death, she found herself actively involved in every facet of the business when she undertook running it on her own. She became very effective in her recruiting because she so thoroughly believed that other families could benefit from an association with Amway in the same manner that her family did.

"When I recruit other women," Bernice says, "I emphasize how wonderful this business has been to our family. You can imagine how this influences their thinking, because women are so security-conscious. Another thing, I point out how family-oriented our business is, and that the wife always knows what's going on because she's working right alongside her husband. In other businesses, the wife is left in the dark, and I believe that leaves her feeling very insecure. With Amway, she has a very clear understanding of the business and can step right in if she suddenly becomes a widow. As a matter of fact, I went back to work very shortly after Fred's funeral because that's the way he would have wanted it. After all, he didn't build this business only to have it stop growing when he was no longer around.

"If you believe in what you're doing as strongly as I do," she explains, "it gives you the self-confidence to convince others to think along the same track. When I talk to another woman and tell her that this is the greatest business in the world, there's no doubt that she knows how much I mean it. You know, people can *sense* this kind of confidence, and you've got to have it in order to be effective in selling.

"The same thing applies in the actual selling of our products. When we first began selling the food supplement products, we firmly believed how beneficial they were. As a matter of fact, I believe in them so much, I still use them to this very day, and to my knowledge, so do Jay and Rich. Even though we were selling a plan which cost $19.50 per month back in 1950, which would be equivalent to around $60 per month today, when you take into account the price increases in food over the years, we sold a lot of Nutrilite *because we believed in it!*

"And that's what makes selling Amway products so easy for me," she continues. "We've got these wonderful products that everyone needs, and they're priced so competitively *you've got to be able to sell them!* We have such a large product line today that there's bound to be several items which you strongly believe in, and if that's true, you're going to have the self-confidence to get out there and generate enthusiasm in your customers. And, boy, that enthusiasm is a contagious thing!"

Although it can easily be understood why Bernice has so much self-confidence today with the fruits of success she has enjoyed with Amway, she is quick to point out that a positive mental attitude was necessary in the early days of the Hansens' selling career. "Fred and I were very fortunate to be able to work closely under the wings of Rich and Jay" Bernice recalls. "We believed in everything they told us, and consequently we followed their instructions to the letter. I can recall them telling us to make twenty calls every day, and if we did, we would end up with three or four interviews, and probably sell one of them. Well, it worked out exactly as they told us.

"Fred initially did the selling and I did the office work, because when we first began, I was stuck at home with a nine-month-old baby. I remember the first day that I finally went out in the field to actually sell. Fred took me to the Cuyahoga Falls area, and he worked one side of the street while I worked the other side. I called on a lovely woman who invited me to sit on the front porch. Her son was quite active in sports, and so she wanted him to have some extra vitamins and minerals. I remember that I was so nervous my pen fell off the porch, so I had to borrow hers to write up the order. That was my very first sale! I was so excited that when I saw Fred coming out of a house across the street, I yelled to him, 'Hey Fred, I got one! How many have you sold?' Well, he didn't have any so he just told me to be quiet.

"When I first started, I called mostly on prospects who were referred by friends. Very shortly after I began selling, a friend of mine who was an old schoolteacher gave me the names of thirty-seven friends. Well, I sold every one of them. What happened was that whenever I didn't sell one, she would call them up and then send me back again. Well, these people respected her and did everything she told them to do. I can't begin to tell you how good this experience was for my confidence as a novice salesperson.

"I am a big believer in rewards," Bernice says, "and when I was out in the field selling, I used to reward myself when I did a good job. In those days, women's hats were very popular, so if I had a good day, I'd go out and buy a hat. I'd always think of some extra little incentive.

"Of course, I guess I learned that from Jay and Rich. They always provided us with extra incentives, which were in the form of bonuses, gifts, awards, trips, and perhaps the most important of all, *recognition!* Amway has many pin awards which are presented to their distributors at different levels. They are: Ruby,

Pearl, Emerald, Diamond, Double Diamond, Triple Diamond, Crown, and Crown Ambassador. [Only one distributorship has made Crown Ambassador as of this writing, and during the next fiscal year, Bernice's distributorship is on target for this goal.] Because we are such a closely knit group, there's a lot of friendly competition to work for the recognition which these different levels represent. In fact, some people say we work for the pins instead of the money.'' Bernice chuckles.

One notices the sparkle in Bernice's eyes as she proudly describes the incentive programs that Amway offers to its people. ''A good example of how motivated we are so we can be recognized within the Amway organization is how hard we worked to qualify for a seminar in Europe recently. It's not that we couldn't afford to pay our own way to Europe if we wanted to go there, it's simply a matter of wanting to go with that group. And to have the recognition which goes with it! You see,'' she asserts positively, ''Amway is a very goal-oriented company and is always establishing goals for its people. The pin awards and the trips are targets which give us directions to aim for. Everyone needs direction, and that's what a goal, whether it's short-term or long-term, provides.

''I can recall our early days with Jay and Rich, when Fred and I had our hearts set on being a key agent with Nutrilite. We had to generate $30,000 worth of business in a period of one month; however, we were $200 short. After we had sent the report in, we sat around for twenty days waiting to hear whether or not we would be recognized as a key agent. Finally they contacted us and said that since we were only $200 short, if Rich and Jay would give their approval, they would give us credit for the full $30,000. Well, we called Rich and Jay and asked them to make an exception since we came so very close, being a mere $200 shy of $30,000. They said, 'No. Either you make it or you don't.' Well, that was one of the best lessons in leadership we ever got!

''Fred and I became so discouraged from our disappointment that our sales volume dropped to one-third of what it had been. We allowed ourselves to be defeated and so did our people. Soon we got a call from Grand Rapids and were told that they were taking bets up there on when we would drop right out of the business. They said that many people quit after a disappointment like ours, and we probably would too.

"Well, I have to admit that phone call made us determined to show them that the Hansens weren't quitters. . . . I guess that's the Irish in me. Fred and I decided that if we couldn't depend upon our people to generate the sales, then we would have to do more retailing ourselves in order to get the business back up there again. When we started to set the pace by showing our people how we were selling, our whole group bounced back. A few months later, we made key agent, and Rich and Jay sent us a telegram saying, 'Well, this time you *really* made it. Congratulations.' "

Bernice looks serious as she philosophizes. "Life is full of disappointments, but the secret of success is to set goals, and then go out to accomplish them. So many people never set any goals because they're afraid they won't accomplish them and there will be grave disappointment. I believe that you always learn something from your disappointments, and consequently you become stronger, not weaker. In our experience, I would say that in 75 percent of the cases where we didn't reach a goal the first time we attempted it, we made it the second time around. And it's so much easier the second time—you have a head start."

Bernice admits that there were times when she felt slightly depressed, but she would never allow it to last more than a few minutes. "I used to give myself pep talks"—she smiles—"I mean it. Whenever I would get into my car, I'd actually talk out loud to myself in order to get myself feeling up. Another thing I did was read a lot of books on positive thinking. I would always have one or two that I would be reading at a time. I would keep them in my car, and if I needed to I'd pull out a book and read a few pages until I felt positive.

"I believe that a negative person who studies books on positive thinking over and over will soon become positive through sheer repetition. That's right, by reading these motivational books again and again, you'll soon condition yourself to think positively. It really works.''

The fact that Bernice would not allow herself to react in a negative fashion has had much to do with her success. ''You've just got to accept those disappointments along the way,'' she explains. ''If you allow yourself to accept defeat, then you *become defeated*. We worked very hard because we knew that there was a certain price which had to be paid for success, and we were willing to pay it. Perhaps the most disappointing thing in this business is when you put a lot of time and energy into sponsoring somebody and then they let you down. Well, when that happens, you just have to shrug your shoulders and go on to the next person.

''I know that when I put my best efforts into somebody and he or she fails,'' Bernice goes on, ''then that person has failed, not me. It's their fault, not mine. They simply weren't willing to pay the price that was demanded of them to succeed, that's all.

''The trouble with most people in the sales field is that they let other people's reactions upset them. For example, they take it too personally when a prospect rejects them or gives them a hassle. I never let a rejection upset me. I always believed that if I did my best job in presenting my products to a customer, and he or she still didn't buy, then at least I was able to educate that individual, and so I performed a service. If I could teach them something about food supplements—and believe me, I'm not a fanatic on the subject—then my visit with the prospect was valuable *even though it didn't result in a sale!* And the same thing was true when I presented any of our household or personal-care products.

''I never felt like I was failing if I didn't get an order. I just figured that the prospect didn't understand, that's all. If he or she did, then there would have had to be a sale. It's as simple as that!

''Like I said, so many people let other people's reactions get to them.'' Bernice shakes her head. ''I can remember when Fred and I first started in this business and our well-intentioned friends and relatives would say to us, 'What kind of business are you going into? Selling vitamins door-to-door!' If we would have listened to them, we would never have gone into this wonderful business. And there was even one relative who bought our food supplement plan and never used it. While he thought he was doing us a favor, it made us feel we were accepting charity when we found out that he never even used it, and that was downright demoralizing! Like I say, most people allow those negative thoughts from uninformed people to upset and discourage them.''

Bernice is such a positive thinker that just being around her makes you catch her attitude. You know exactly what she means when she says, ''The only people I associate with are positive. I don't even like to be around anyone with a negative attitude. Of course, it's very easy to be negative. Being positive is something you have to work at. But when you stop to consider how much it influences your entire life, it's definitely worth whatever effort it requires.

''My philosophy is for each of us to enjoy each day that we're alive, and as one chapter in our life closes, then we have a new one to face.''

The Hansen family's association with Amway has been more than just a chapter of their lives. It's been a durable relationship, filled with admiration, enthusiasm, and success. It began at a time in their lives when they had nothing but a strong will to succeed. The ambitious couple had moved from Grand Rapids to Ohio with three young children and Bernice's elderly parents. They had no savings in the bank, but what they did possess was a positive mental attitude and a golden opportunity. It's the great American dream for a husband and wife to pick themselves up by the bootstraps and acquire wealth and security, not to mention a tremendous sense of accomplishment. For Bernice Hansen it wasn't only a dream. As they say at Amway, ''It's the American way.''

4

Francis G. ("Buck") Rodgers

(IBM)

"Striving for excellence..."

Francis ("Buck") Rodgers is vice president of marketing for the International Business Machines Corporation. He joined the company in Cleveland, Ohio, in 1950. In 1957, following various marketing assignments, he was named administrative assistant to the executive vice president of IBM.

Buck graduated from Miami University (Ohio) in 1950 with a major in industrial management and marketing. After a variety of field marketing and headquarters staff positions, such as branch manager, regional sales manager, and director of finance. industry programs, he was named president of the IBM data processing division in 1967. In October 1970, he was appointed IBM director of marketing, with overall worldwide marketing responsibilities. He was elected vice president of marketing in June, 1974.

He is a trustee of the Marketing Science Institute at Harvard University, Woodrow Wilson Visiting Fellow, director of the Sales Executive Club of New York, member of the Business Advisory Council of Miami University, member of the United Nations/ Industry Cooperative Programme, member of the Advisory Council of the University of Tennessee, and is active in a wide variety of civic organizations. He has headed IBM United Way campaigns as well as its bond programs.

Buck spends a great deal of time lecturing on college campuses and to civic and business organizations. He estimates that he delivers twenty-five or more speeches every year in support of the free-enterprise system and the fact that rewards, excitement, and ethics do exist in the business world.

He is a dedicated jogger who runs several miles a day. He's a low handicap golfer and an avid tennis player.

He and his wife, Helen, live in Darien, Connecticut. They have three children: Christy, twenty-five; Scott, twenty-four; and Kathy, twenty-three.

It has been said that IBM is the most important company in history. Millions of people are in some way affected by the company's tremendous contribution to our society, a contribution which reaches every corner of our planet, and even beyond the earth's atmosphere. And, for the record, it is the author's opinion that IBM's contributions to society in the next fifty or so years will be far greater than those to date.

IBM's technological achievements have been truly remarkable, but its marketing accomplishments are equally impressive. The two really go hand in hand. In a free-enterprise system, no matter how superior a product may be, unless a company goes into the marketplace and sells its wares, nothing will be accomplished.

Francis ("Buck") Rodgers' job is marketing IBM's products. He is the vice president of marketing—in a company with a worldwide sales team of more than 70,000 people in direct selling, systems engineering, and supportive roles. Buck's job includes the marketing of all IBM products, ranging from magnetic tapes and copiers to typewriters and computer systems. IBM's revenues from sales, rentals, and services in 1976 were $16.8

FRANCIS G. (''BUCK'') RODGERS

billion. The marketing organization Buck oversees has been called the finest in the world.

People marvel at Rodgers' huge responsibility. And many are under the impression that there's a certain mystique about a computer, IBM's most widely recognized product. ''That's a fallacy,'' Buck insists. ''We simply supply a solution to our customers' problems. We're not selling a product, but instead what the product will do.

''For example,'' Buck explains, ''if I walk into your office and say, 'I've got something that's going to make your job easier, it's going to reduce your cost, and it's a way to allow you to give better service to your customers,' you're going to be interested in hearing what I've got to tell you. And that's what it's all about!

''While there are people who fear a computer and think in terms of its impersonal nature, you've got to look at what the machine actually does. It can help save lives, for example, when used in medicine. It can mechanize our libraries and make them more useful. It can aid in the decision process. It can free people from repetitive work. It can make somebody's job more exciting and more meaningful. There are, in fact, countless ways a computer can serve mankind.''

As Buck explains the many uses of the computer, he rises from his seat, gesturing enthusiastically as he paces back and forth. ''So we speak in terms of what the customer's problems are, and how we're going to solve them. We consider IBM to be in the business of information processing, but more important, we're in the business of satisfying customers. To me, the basis of marketing is to find a way to create a customer and then to keep him!''

When you listen to Buck explain such a seemingly complicated business as the computer industry by breaking it down into understandable selling concepts, it doesn't seem nearly so involved after all. This is particularly true when he talks about the principles that influence IBM's every action, as they did when Tom Watson, Sr., began the company in 1914.

''In order to understand IBM,'' Buck declares, ''you must understand the three basic beliefs which give substance to whatever we do. First is respect for the individual. Second, a long time ago we decided that we would give the best service of any company in the world. And third, we expect superior performance in what our people do. By this we mean that we expect nothing less than excellence." As T. J. Watson, Sr., used to put it, "It is better to aim at perfection and miss than it is to aim at imperfection and hit it."

"Isn't it mandatory that for an organization to stay on top, it must pursue all tasks with the clear understanding that they can be accomplished in an outstanding manner? Insistence on excellence leads groups to tackle almost impossible tasks. As a result, something develops within a company that might be called a 'tone.' It is a blend of optimism, enthusiasm, excitement, and pace.

"T. J. Watson, Jr., former IBM chairman of the board, has summed up the company's philosophy this way: 'It is IBM's credo that any organization, in order to survive and to achieve success, must have a sound set of beliefs on which it bases all its policies and actions. But more important than having a set of beliefs is faithful adherence to those beliefs. If any organization is to meet the challenges of a changing world, it must be prepared to change everything about itself except those beliefs as it moves through its present to its future. Let me reiterate. The basic philosophy, the very spirit and drive of an organization, has far more to do with its relative achievements than do technological or economic resources, organizational structure, innovation and timing.'

"Sure," says Buck, "all of these things weigh heavily in success, but they are brought into being by how strongly the people in the organization believe in what they are doing and how willingly they execute their responsibilities. At IBM, beliefs always come before policies, practices, and goals. The latter must always be altered if they are seen to violate fundamental beliefs. The only sacred cow in an organization should be its basic philosophy of doing business."

Buck Rodgers' personal business philosophy is a reflection of

IBM's. This is quite natural, as his entire career since his graduation from college in 1950 has been with the company. He began in the company's electric typewriter division in Cleveland, and one year later moved over to data processing, which at the time was called the "electronic accounting machine division." In Cleveland, Buck concentrated on manufacturing accounts, selling punch card accounting machines. He later sold computers. In 1956, he was transferred to Youngstown, Ohio, to handle the Westinghouse Electric Company account in Sharon, Pennsylvania, where IBM installed one of the first large-scale computers in the country. Following that assignment, he was transferred to the corporate headquarters as an administrative assistant to an executive vice president.

After moving through a series of field marketing jobs, including branch managerial positions, Buck went into industry marketing. For three years, he headed IBM's banking, brokerage, and financial section, and then was appointed sales manager for the data processing division in the U.S. Eastern region. He next spent five years in Los Angeles heading the West Coast operations, and was made a vice president of the computer division. In 1967, Buck was elected president of the data processing division, IBM's largest division, which markets and services the company's computer systems in the United States. After three years, he was appointed IBM director of marketing on a worldwide basis. In 1974, he was elected IBM vice president.

IBM's simple concept of respect for the individual occupies a major portion of management time and effort. IBM prides itself on offering continual opportunities for advancement. Of course, many of these opportunities are a result of the company's rapid growth. No matter how great the temptation to recruit outside the company, with rare exception IBM has filled key positions by promoting from within. A few top scientists, lawyers, and other specialists have been hired, but nearly all the other executives came up through the ranks. This system has played a major role in the high morale of the company. Buck Rodgers is an outstanding example of how at IBM an individual can have a modest beginning to his or her career, but through performance and desire can rise to a high management level.

"In order to fully understand IBM's second principle," Buck says, "striving to give the best service in the world, it is important to understand the emphasis placed on training and developing individuals. Our training program ranges from four months to approximately eighteen months depending on the division. During this period, we spend a great deal of time orienting that person to what the IBM company is like. We emphasize product knowledge, and we relate specifics so he or she will understand what the product can or cannot do.

"For example, in our data processing division, during the first month of training our computer salesperson will spend a month observing in a branch office. This will involve making calls with our people and seeing what marketing and IBM is all about. After that first month, the recruitee goes to an education center. There are education centers throughout the United States, located for example, in Chicago, Dallas, San Jose, and Atlanta. We also have headquarters education centers which provide additional support. Following the session at the education center, the trainee spends another month or two in the branch office, observing actual situations and using the knowledge already acquired. Then a return to the formal education center to receive more in-depth training. Then back to the branch office for further application.

"So, it's practice complemented with theory," Buck emphasizes. "Then the trainee goes on to the final class, which features simulated sales situations. There he learns how to operate in a territory, what to expect from a customer, and how to do a thorough account plan. As you can see, by the time anyone has finished our training program, he or she has complete product knowledge, knows how to apply it, and has spent several weeks going through demonstrations in front of other salespersons. When that person gets into a live situation in front of a real customer, it's not going to be foreign to him or her.

"Another very important thing we do at IBM is specialize our sales force according to a given industry. It's difficult for a salesman to walk down the street and call on an insurance company, then a small manufacturer, and finish by making a call on a retail store. So we specialize our data processing sales force according to industry knowledge. There are about fifteen major industry classifications; these are broken down into subsets. For example, there's retail, insurance, manufacturing, and so forth. But, within the transportation classification, there's motor freight, airlines, and railroads. A salesman or a branch office may deal only with retail companies, another only with supermarkets. One may specialize in banks, another in savings and loans.

"The key thing to note is that our people are trained to be experts in given areas. They can go to a prospect and speak his language. They understand his problems because they're familiar with his business. Again, we're not selling a product, but instead what that product will do. As I said before, when an IBM salesperson calls on a customer, he or she must offer something in the way of a constructive suggestion. We're in a highly competitive world, and there are some very fine companies who can build good equipment. So the secret becomes how to tailor a system to a customer's specific needs. By specializing according to industry, a salesperson is going to be knowledgeable about the customer, and only with this kind of knowledge can the business be obtained.''

The high standards IBM has established for developing quality personnel are inseparable from the company's quest for giving the best possible service to the customer. ''We're looking for people who have the ability to relay ideas and to seek out solutions,'' Buck asserts. ''In addition to fully preparing the individual to service the customer, we believe in measuring our people to make certain that they're meeting some very tough sales objectives and marketing targets. It's important to reward success and penalize failure, as long as the individual has been forewarned that his performance is not up to par. We find that people want to be measured.

"Every individual in the IBM Corporation is given an objective to achieve, and he or she is appraised every year and told very clearly of his or her overall performance. If the person isn't performing up to standards, well, we obviously don't want inefficient people operating in a sales territory.''

Buck smiles. ''I find that people today want to be told why, not how. They want to have a challenging objective, and as long as the management of the business displays an interest in them and rewards them for what they accomplish, a certain esprit de corps develops. This, I believe, is a very positive thing. With our marketing people, we spend a great deal of time in territory definition so we can put together the right target for that particular individual. It's very important to be thorough in your marketing research, so you can correctly project the proper sales quota. If a quota is too easy, your salesman isn't living up to his expectation and you're not getting the full potential out of him. Consequently, your revenue will suffer. On the other hand, if it's an unachievable quota, he may end up not giving the customer the right level of service.

''You see, we expect excellence in what our people do, but this must go beyond the articulation of words. A company must have programs. Examples must be set for its people to follow. For instance, when we speak about respect for the individual it should be noted that when we find we have surplus people due to technology change, we will go to great lengths to retrain those individuals and find them meaningful assignments. We have a full employment practice at IBM and work hard to maintain it.

''I guess it really boils down to communications with your people. The line manager has to keep in close contact with the salesperson, and must often sit down with him or her at the end of the day and say, 'Tell me about what went on in the territory,' Then, he might suggest, 'Hey, I would like to make a call with you tomorrow and see if I can offer some assistance.'

''Now in order to be able to effectively accomplish the right kind of communications,'' Buck adds, ''a company must have a realistic employee-manager relationship. For example, we think that a company should have one manager for about every ten salespersons. And every salesperson should know very clearly that the manager has knowledge of day-to-day activities. At IBM we have 'executive interviews' whereby every year we expect a manager from a level above the individual's immediate management to sit down with him and discuss just how things are going. We also have an 'executive resources program' that asks managers at all levels to identify the truly outstanding performers. Also, when we promote a person, the manager taking that action must identify future levels of responsibility. In addition, there are always at least three or four candidates considered for every job that comes up. This is a comprehensive selection system that is based on performance rather than who you know. It's a highly competitive process, but it works because we have good people.''

As one makes an in-depth analysis of IBM's great marketing success, what emerges is the teamwork of the entire company's resources mobilized to provide the best possible service for the customer. Of course, this starts with quality people throughout the whole organization, a must if a quality product is to be the end result. But, as important as the quality of the product is the servicing of the customer after the sale is made.

"When you get right down to it," Buck states, "it means that you have to understand the difference between selling and marketing. Selling is the art of persuasion where you utilize your individual talents to convince someone to buy the product or service you offer. Marketing, however, is a much more inclusive term which means understanding the customer's business and putting together a solution to his problems, thereby increasing his productivity. You're constantly looking for ways for your products to serve him better, so he, in turn, can better serve his customer. Of course, everything you do for him must be cost-justified, and he has to get a realistic return on his investment. In other words, you're giving him value, and the end result will be a satisfied customer. Naturally, when you've got a satisfied customer, your company is going to end up with higher revenue and growth.

"When we talk about marketing, we're speaking in terms of

using every resource within a business. I consider our engineering organization, for example, to be marketing-oriented because they're continually trying to come up with some unique feature or some difference in the product itself. Likewise, I consider our manufacturing people to be part of this effort to market our products because they're constantly trying to increase quality and lower costs. Everyone in some capacity is related to marketing at IBM; even the people on the switchboard and our administrative people help us to service the customer. You see, we're an organization which is market-driven.''

The trim six-foot-one Rodgers, who looks much younger than his fifty-one years, rises and walks to the front of his desk. Again gesturing to make his point, he says, ''There is a whole series of steps and processes that a salesperson has to go through, whether it's selling an IBM product or, for that matter, anything else, so let me go through the process. First, you've got to develop an interest on the part of the customer and make him aware that you're trying to be of service to him. At IBM, we think it's important that a partnership be developed so the customer realizes there's something more than just a one-time-call situation. Over a period of time, the salesman can go in and develop an understanding of the customer, so that the salesman can put together a plan that has substance over a several-year period.

''In order to plan meaningfully, a team of marketing and technical people will go out for a week or two and put together a plan which will lay out the equipment needed and applications to be installed as well as a cost/benefit recommendation covering several years. This plan is then presented to the customer, and that is where the partnership comes into play. When you get the company and the customer working together, then he thinks of you not as an IBMer but as one of his people, as if you were on his payroll. When you do that, you're achieving the highest level of customer satisfaction that you possibly can. You and the customer are working together toward a common objective.

''Once the salesperson demonstrates to the customer that a need exists, then the salesperson tries to put together the best solution. From the solution stage you have to figure the best set of products to solve that particular problem. This means going through some very nitty-gritty work, such as understanding the actual process in which, let's say, a sales order is handled. The salesperson must be able to determine how the customer establishes his inventory levels. If it's a manufacturing operation, he needs to be able to understand how shop orders are prepared and how people on the shop floor interface with the scheduling department. Once these volumes are determined, and that entails a very detailed analysis, the salesperson puts together a proposal which is documented in detail with all the processes he's studied, and provides step-by-step answers to the specific problems. Hopefully, from that, the salesperson can show the customer that the solution is cost-justified and the order is closed.

"But this is just the beginning," Buck continues. "With IBM, nothing is successfully sold until it's successfully installed. Now the salesperson goes through the installation phase, including educating the customer, teaching his people how the products will actually perform, and showing him how to properly apply the product. Finally, the equipment is delivered; this can be almost a year later. At any rate, that's the installation phase of the sale.

"Beyond that, we take it much further. We're dealing with a customer on a continual basis, for example, trying to find new applications to further justify the equipment. At IBM, we're often leasing a fairly expensive piece of equipment, and unless we continue to give the customer the best possible service, always looking out for his best interest, we're taking the risk of losing him.

"We're big believers in preventive maintenance, and we think that's one of the keys to success at IBM. It involves not just the sales organization, but also the people who are actually keeping the equipment operating day by day. We have the capacity to respond in any part of the country and any part of the world. That's why when we say, 'IBM means service,' we're including engineering, manufacturing, administration, customer engineering, and selling.''

Buck shakes his head. "Today in some industries, marketing people unfortunately really don't demonstrate a true customer interest. For instance, you can walk into a new car dealership's showroom and many times can't find anybody who can tell you anything about the product, let alone convey the fact that they're trying to give you a better means of transportation. I don't want to pick on the automobile industry"—Buck smiles—"but, how many times have you walked into a showroom and nobody even bothered to say hello to you! Not only should a car salesman walk up and say, 'Hello, can I help you?' but he should be sure to point out features in addition to how comfortably the car rides. He should show you how the model's economy can save you money, and he should make sure that you clearly understand the advantages of the engine from a reliability aspect. Also, after a car is sold, how many times have you ever had a formal follow-up by the dealer to remind you to bring it in for preventive maintenance? The auto agency doesn't just exist on the basis of selling cars; it's also dependent upon the repair shop to generate extra revenue. It's almost as if most salespeople have lost interest in offering what we refer to as excellence in service. It's a shame, but in almost any field when you get good service it's an exception, and you're excited about it. It ought to be the other way around.

"At IBM, we believe that an order is never certified or achieved until a system is successfully installed. You see, it's a continuing type of process. We use both internal sources and outside surveys to measure customer satisfaction. At IBM, we have market requirement statements that indicate what products are needed by our customers based on what they say is required, rather than what an engineer off in a corner somewhere feels that technology should provide. We never let up in providing the best possible service to our customer. It's an ongoing thing.

"Repeat business!" Buck slams his fist on his desktop to emphasize his point. "And that's why we say to our sales force, 'Getting the order may be the easiest thing of all, even though you had to go through this long process of justification.' But since a lot of our equipment is leased, it's only going to stay with the customer as long as we keep him satisfied. So the salesperson must keep going back to that customer saying, 'Here's a new product. Here's a new technique. Here's a new application. Here's something I think may save you an hour on the machine.' And, boy, is this follow-up activity important! No matter how small it may seem. Those little things make a big, big difference. And because it's a continuing process, we use two words together: 'Sell-Install,' never one without the other. At IBM we say, 'Nothing is ever sold until it's properly installed; nothing is ever installed until it's properly sold.'

"You know," Buck continues, "It's easy for a salesperson to get enthusiastic when a product is sold and he does a fine job of it. But it's equally important to have the same attitude and tend to the little things, too. For example, if there's a meeting that he has to attend with a customer, he'd better make sure that he's going to be there—and on time, too. Or perhaps a customer asked for some information, maybe some brochures. Well, the salesperson had better make it his business to see that the customer gets what he asked for. Another little thing which too many salesmen neglect to do is to promptly return calls from their customers. These things help to develop a relationship of mutual trust. Pretty soon, everything just seems to fall into place. The salesperson has pride in his work, and the customer seeing that has confidence in the salesperson because he knows that he or she has self-confidence. And I don't care what the product is, belief in oneself is basic in selling. It's what sells products!"

Buck Rodgers has plenty of self-confidence himself. You can sense it in the air when you're in the same room with him. "At IBM," he says, "we develop self-confidence in our people because we prepare them very well before they make the first call on a customer. Just the other day I was talking with a young person who was thinking about a career with IBM. I asked if he thought he could sell. He answered, 'If I believe in the product and I understand what the product can do, I can sell it.' That's a pretty good lesson to learn no matter what field you're in. I've seen many salesmen who really didn't know their product, but instead relied on such things as showmanship or price alone. Well, in today's competitive world, you're going to lose if that's all you've got. That feeling of self-confidence comes partly from how much a person is willing to learn on his own and partly how well the company trains him.

"There are two things in the business that we say ought to be increased out of proportion to the growth rate of the business. Number one is education and training, and number two is communications. We spend a lot of time telling people *why* instead of *how*. And most of us have a tendency to tell people how they ought to do it, but not *why*.

"As I said before, we expect excellence in what our people do. But, you can't just talk about those things, you've got to practice them. And you try to do that through personal leadership, through those appraisal programs and all the things that go with them.

"We train our people to ask for the order. It's no secret why you are calling on the person—it's to sell something. If a salesman really believes in his product, and he knows that the product will benefit a customer, then he should ask for the order."

While IBM has instituted an educational system for developing its people, the company has also designed a program for educating its customers. Customer education centers are located throughout the United States; in addition, there are fifty in foreign countries. "Between educating our peole and our customers"—Buck smiles—"we're figuratively the largest university in the world.

"We spend a lot of time orienting our customers, from the top executives down through the system programmers and the people who will actually be operating the machines. At IBM, for example, we run a chief executive class for the presidents and chief executive officers often of billion-dollar-or-more corporations. They'll come into our headquarters and spend a week or so with us becoming oriented to what's new in technology and what's happening in the field of computers. More important, we try to tell them how a computer system can be a tool in the decision-making process, and how that computer can help increase their productivity or improve their services.

"Another project is conducted in conjunction with the Harvard Business School. We want our salesmen to feel comfortable with top executives, so we believe they should understand how those executives think. Our account executives and large account managers spend approximately three weeks taking courses heavily oriented to financial planning, organization, and how a company actually operates.

"At Rutgers University, in another typical program, our people take a curriculum geared to helping them understand the banking industry. We believe that every salesman must be able to understand what the customer is doing. If he doesn't, there's no way to give him an adequate answer for a particular problem. We believe every salesman ought to present an intelligent long-term account plan. We do this not only because we sell products which aid the planning process, but because we believe that unless you understand the forces that are having the greatest influence on your business, then these forces will control you rather than the other way around. So we develop scenarios of the marketplace, where we determine what changes are going to take place in a given industry, and we attempt to convey this information to our sales force. Then, when salespersons go to a customer, they're idea-oriented and they have something constructive to present. Of course, this doesn't happen every time, but this is what we strive for.

"As part of IBM's customer awareness program, every customer complaint to any of the company's branch offices or corporate headquarters will be acknowledged within a twenty-four-hour period. This doesn't mean that we will have the answer, but at least we say to the customer via phone call, wire, or letter that we are working on the problem. One of the best ads we ever ran simply stated, *IBM Means Service*. If our people aren't giving service, we'll take corrective action immediately."

Buck continues. "We believe in selling our strengths, not someone else's weaknesses. Therefore, when a customer asks one of our people for an opinion on a competitive product, our answer is, 'I'll tell you what our product will do and how we can provide the finest in service, but under no set of circumstances do we ever disparage or knock someone else.' We have a very clear policy on this, and if anyone disparages competitive people or products, they will be subject to the most severe disciplinary action.

"Again, it's a concept of simply being fair and following fundamental business ethics. Everybody should have an opportunity to present openly what he has to offer, so that free enterprise prevails and whoever has the finest in service and quality of product will win."

It's truly remarkable for a corporation with a gross income in excess of $16 billion and assets of approximately $18 billion to have such a posture, but IBM is a unique company. "We're always fighting size," Buck insists, "and we're constantly looking for new ways to become more responsive. Divisionalization is often the answer, but more important, it's the attitude of our people. We try to keep our branch offices at a size where no one individual gets lost and at the same time where we can maintain direct communications with our customers.

"Although IBM is one of the largest companies in the world, we don't think that size is the important thing to stress. When we were small, we didn't make an issue of it, and when we grew, we never stressed anything to do with being big. What we have stressed all along is that we're responsive. We're a company that's light on its feet. We're a company which is made up of individuals. We're a company with an umbrella over it that says, 'We're striving for excellence in what we do.' All along, we have stressed quality and service.

"We are saying to our customers, 'IBM is interested in you, and you can judge us on that basis.' You know when you look at IBM, or for that matter other big companies, there are two sides to the question of bigness. To some, where individual service is poor, bigness can indicate bureaucracy, with the customer feeling that you don't really have his best interest at heart. The other type of reputation, and the one that a market-driven company wants, is that this company has excellent resources, good people, and they do the little things well.''

Since Tom Watson, Sr., established certain principles for his company, the management, led by men like Buck Rodgers, has worked hard at maintaining them. It is a reflection of these principles that has enabled the company to keep its integrity while doing business on a worldwide scale. That's quite an achievement for any company, let alone one the size of IBM.

5

Shelby H. Carter, Jr.

(XEROX)

"A matter of pride..."

Shelby H. Carter, Jr., is senior vice president of Xerox Corporation's Information Systems Group and vice president of the corporation. He is the senior vice president of U.S. field operations for sales, service, and administration of all Xerox copier and duplicator products and supplies sold in the United States.

Shelby joined Xerox in January 1970 as regional sales manager for the company's northeast region. He later became the national sales manager for industry marketing, was named vice president and national sales manager in March 1972, and vice president, systems marketing staff, in 1973. He was named vice president for field operations in January 1975, and senior vice president in January 1976. In January 1977, he was elected a corporate vice president.

Shelby was born on March 23, 1931, in Brooklyn, New York. He graduated from the University of Texas with a bachelor of business administration degree, and he also attended the Law School at the University of Texas for one year. He later studied law at the University of Maryland. From 1953 to 1956, he was a first lieutenant in the Marine Corps serving his last two years as aide-de-camp to the commanding general of the Second Marine Division.

Prior to joining Xerox, Shelby spent fourteen years in marketing and line management positions with the International Business Machines Corporation. He now lives with his wife, Patricia, who is a teacher, in Rochester, New York. They have six children: Shelby III, twenty-three; Randy, twenty-two; Michael, twenty; Jane, seventeen; Colin, fourteen; and Dan, eleven.

Shelby has served on boards for various civic and business activities and is an avid jogger and tennis player.

During a five-day trip to fifteen Xerox branch offices, Shelby Carter repeatedly gave his field people the following message:

> We're not going to hamstring you. We're not going to send you out there without the necessary tools. I don't like eating my teeth any more than you do.
>
> We're going to give you a realistic, achievable game plan to follow. In the last couple of years, I've been reading in the business and financial magazines—and I know they're right—that the Xerox marketing force is the best around. Well, now we're going to have a chance to prove it *again*. I'm going to ask you to carry the back quarter of this year the way you've never been asked before. It's in your hands now.

His message is positive, and clearly tells them exactly what he wants and expects them to do. He generates enthusiasm and excitement when he speaks. He's proud to be a super sales personality, and his pride is contagious. Shelby Carter makes everybody in the room want to do his or her very best. He won't allow them to settle for anything less.

It takes an individual like Shelby, who's been there himself, to motivate a sales force in such a positive way. He's not telling anyone to do anything he hasn't already done himself. He thrives

SHELBY H. CARTER, JR.

on being a salesman, and it's this pride that makes him so effective with his people.

"I'm very proud of salesmanship," he says with a broad smile. "I think it's an American heritage. I enjoy going out and seeing customers, and to this day, I keep in touch with what they need and want by going out in the trenches with my troops. I call on customers across the country. It's something I love, and I'll continue to do it as long as I'm involved in marketing."

Since a three-year stint in the Marines, Shelby's entire career has been sales-oriented, and he glows with the enthusiasm of an eager new sales representative starting off in his first territory. "When you're pounding pavement with what I used to refer to as a canvas rock," he cracks, "you've got to be tough. When I started selling IBM typewriters in 1956, I had a sign placed on my car's visor which read, 'Calls are the guts of this business.' We lived in Baltimore, and I used to drive forty miles every day just to get to Annapolis, which was part of my territory. My wife, Pat, used to fix me a big jug of lemonade, which I kept in the back of my car so I wouldn't have to stop for lunch. But, boy, you have to be tough on yourself. You've got to make that extra call. I tell my salespeople today, 'You make one more call a day, and that's five a week, twenty a month, and two hundred and forty calls a year. Now what good Xerox person can't close 10 percent? And if you get another twenty-four sales a year, you've got to be a winner!'

"The sales managers are the people who set the pace," explains Shelby. "They have to show the way. They have to draw on that discipline. And I don't care what you're selling. It could be typewriters, insurance, real estate, anything. If you get those extra calls in, say an extra twenty per month, you're going to get three demos, and one will result in a sale.

"But one thing you have to realize, while that leadership role is important, it doesn't mean that everybody will automatically follow their leader. What I really think is important to understand is the fact that sales reps only work for one person. Themselves! I don't care what all the psychologists and psychiatrists in the world say. When sales reps go home at the end of a tough day, they say, 'Damn it, I got mine!' Yeah, 'I got *mine* today!' It's a tough, hard world, and when you go into the heart of Manhattan, L.A., or Chicago, and find somebody who doesn't believe that, well, I'll tell you, you got yourself a problem.

"It's an inner desire; salespeople want to compete," Shelby asserts. "People shouldn't be in sales if they don't have this kind of desire. They don't go home at night and say, 'I got one for Carter today.' Hell, they don't even know me. It's inner pride which drives them to get results, because it makes them feel they're accomplishing something. Sure, after doing it for themselves, they might want to do it for their branch manager. But never forget: They do it for themselves first.

"Of course, when a branch manager becomes personally involved, this closeness will provide great motivation," Shelby continues. "I can remember my first sales manager at IBM, a fellow by the name of Tommy Thompson. Now, here's a great example of leadership. I was making $250 a month in 1956, and about three weeks after my daughter was born, she developed spinal meningitis. She was in the hospital, and I was hard-pressed for the money to pay the bills. Tommy called me into his office and said, 'Look, Carter, I have a dividend check for $500, and I don't know what to do with it. So I'm going to give it to you. . . . Here, take it!' "

Shelby's voice breaks. "I'll never forget Tommy Thompson to the day I die. As I look back now, I say, 'Sure, he didn't know what to do with the check. The son of a gun probably had a million things to do with it.' Now that's what I call involvement—the kind that really makes you want to do a big job for someone who had faith in you."

After a slight pause, Shelby reflects, "You know, a cardinal rule in sales management, when personal involvement with your people is mentioned, is: Stay out of it! But in the real world, you *do* get involved. You live together and you work together. You really get to know your people, and you develop a relationship with them that is a lasting one. Some of my oldest friends are the people I've sold with, and even though I haven't seen some of them for twenty to twenty-five years, my wife and I still keep in contact with them. Maybe it's only a Christmas card, but we really look forward to hearing from them each year.''

With Xerox people, sales training begins with an indoctrination program that starts when a salesperson first meets the company. ''The company has a tape we play for people before we even hire them,'' explains Shelby. ''And we lay the cards right on the table when sales representatives first start their careers with Xerox. We tell them how difficult the job may be. We also tell them that if they run with the team—and we'll teach them the plays—they'll learn to execute what they've been trained to do like a pro football player. Every play is designed to make a touchdown, or in our case a sale. That's right, every play, if done right, theoretically is designed to score. They'll go to our school, and right from the beginning they'll learn the little things, such as that classes start on time.

''We have a process that dictates, 'You've gotta be squared away.' When I'm with a sales rep, I'll constantly look for every last detail to make sure that they're squared away. I'll check little things like their briefcase, and if it's not organized, I'll come right down on top of them! The next thing I want to know is 'Where's the business card?' And if they don't have one, I'll nail them. I want to know every little last detail. Do they have the proper sales literature? Are they well organized? Everything.

''And the whole thing is perpetuated by example. Although it's an unwritten code, I'd estimate that 99.9 percent of our salesmen wear a suit instead of a sports jacket, even though a suit is not required. We've got an image, and it's a very subtle thing. We have a tempo that we set. It's discipline within the organization, and it's the sales reps' inner pride that makes them want to be part of the team. As I said before, 'We're tough,' but it's not a toughness that's brittle or breaks. It's toughness like leather; you've got to be pliable. You've got to be able to bend a little, to give, to be malleable. When you're working with different kinds of people, you have to be able to manage them all a little differently. For example, if a salesman is out in a territory like

Wyoming, he's going to dress differently than the man in Manhattan or Chicago. In the South, it may be perfectly acceptable for a salesman to make a call wearing a short-sleeved shirt and a tie, without the suit jacket.

"I can remember back in the early sixties"—the impeccably dressed Shelby laughs—"when I went up to Boston to work in the field with a young salesman in his mid-twenties. This particular salesman was wearing those long sideburns called 'mutton chops.' Boy, I was really turned off, but I decided not to say anything at first. We made calls on the customers and prospects in his territory, and by the end of the day I realized that 90 percent of the people we called on also wore mutton chops! I imagine that they were sitting there thinking, Say, who's this staid-looking guy with the dark suit, short hair, and funny-looking shoes? (I was wearing my wing-tipped shoes, which I call my shoes with the thousand holes in them.) So you have to be able to make some adjustments. Again, it's back to being tough, but pliable."

Shelby doesn't believe the myth that salespeople are born or that there's such a thing as a model salesperson. "I have a theory on sales people which I call my 'Heinz Fifty-seven Variety' theory." He chuckles. "I could bring you fifty-seven different salesmen within a given company, and they'll all have different personalities. Everything about them may appear to be different, and yet each of them may be successful in his own way. So when I hire salespeople, I have a list of five basic things that I look for. The first thing is whether they are solution-oriented or problem-oriented. I want a person who walks in and instead of telling me what the problems are, I'll get solutions. What good is it to have someone telling you what's wrong if they can't figure out the solutions? And I'll dig right into them by asking all kinds of questions to see how they react. I'll ask, 'How are you going to do it? What's the first thing you're going to do?' Or if they are candidates for management, I'll ask questions such as 'Are you going to have operation meetings every week? What about staff meetings? Why are you going to do it that way?' Then I might just throw in a test question such as 'What would you do if . . .?'

"Next, I want to know if they are willing to pay the cost—I call it commitment. And it comes from desire. Is the person willing to pay the cost that it takes to be successful? Then, I want to know if they are decisive. And before a person can be decisive, are they incisive? Do they think things through? You know, sometimes doing nothing is a good decision. I'll ask such questions as 'Where do you want to be five years from now?' They may reply, 'I want to be a branch manager. I want to be a vice president.' I tell them that if they'll tell me where they want to be, then I'll map it out for them and show them how to get there. If they give you a quick answer without thinking, then they're not being incisive. I like to see them sit back and answer, 'Gee, that's a good question. I hadn't thought about projecting my career for five years. I'd like to separate the issues. I've got some personal ones and some business ones. Let me separate them.' And then I'll sit and chat about them for a few minutes. I like it when they dissect the issues and think them through.''

A serious look appears on Shelby's face as he continues. "There's a key word that goes hand in hand with being decisive. And that word is 'risk.' The quicker a person can make a decision and be right, that's what I want! Whether it's bidding on a major proposal, which may involve a cost analysis and productivity projection, or something which may pertain to their personal life. Perhaps someone might say, 'I don't think I want to work on a commission basis. Why don't you put me on a full salary?' It's those kind of comments that show you what a person has.

"My fourth criterion is one which upsets a lot of people," Shelby admits. "It's being tough but right. I keep coming back to this 'being tough' bit, but only because it's a very critical point. It's a quality that evolves with you through self-discipline. A person really gets in there with an understanding that nothing is going to come easy and he or she has got to work hard for everything in this world. It's part physical, and it's part emotional. Being able to draw on that extra reserve. It all starts with the salesperson out in the street. Making that extra call. Again, I go back to 1956, when I had that sign right on my visor reading, 'Calls are the guts of this business.' And I just kept driving myself. One more call—go after it.''

The trim, youthful-looking sales executive sits back in his chair and ponders: "My last thought is a philosophical one. And, I call it perspective. You've got to be able to find salespersons and managers who can keep everything in perspective. When you talk to energetic people who are aggressive, the biggest thing on their minds is generally the job, and its career opportunities. Now they have to be able to relate importance to other facets of their lives. Don't forget, there's more to life than working. There's the family, community involvement, religion, and a whole bunch of enjoyable things. Now the important thing is: Can they still smile? Can they get away from the job? Or are they so intense they're like the person who wakes up at five o'clock in the morning and just lies in bed and screams out, 'I gotta get up at six!' That's the kind of thing that you have to be careful about.

"Have you ever noticed how many salesmen's trousers are always worn out at the right pocket?" Shelby grins. "It's not because he keeps his wallet in there. The wallet is usually in the back pocket or the left-hand side. It's because before the guy shakes hands with a customer, he's wiping it on his pants. Yeah, I would estimate that 20 to 30 percent of the sales people you shake hands with, and you watch them, are wiping the sweat off their hands before they shake hands. Sure, you've got to have a little of the adrenaline going, so I'm not referring to that. I'm talking about those who are so uptight that they're dying out there. And that's a pity.

"So a salesperson has got to keep everything in its proper perspective. If they press too hard, they get what I call cumulative battle fatigue. If they're not careful, and you know that most salespeople are pretty high-strung and emotional, they just keep grinding away, and then cumulative battle fatigue sets in. Like I said, you can spot them when they rub their clothes before they shake hands.

"You know," Shelby continues, "so many salespeople are so involved in their work that they're actually afraid to say that they're going on vacation. Well, I'll tell you a story. We were having a meeting on 'Management by Example,' and I was winding up my presentation to my entire management team. I told them in my closing speech, 'All right, now that's what we're going to do. Boom, boom, boom . . . now go out and do it.' Then I concluded by telling them, 'I'm going fishin', I'm leaving.' And I took my eleven-year-old son and my fourteen-year-old son to Nantucket for two weeks. Yeah, and the last day, we caught thirteen blues." Shelby laughs.

"Speaking about our 'Management by Example' program," Shelby recalls, "we recently told our management team that everybody would go through what we call 'hands-on training.' Well, we all went down to our Leesburg, Virginia, Training Center, and everybody went through the very basics. I mean everybody—me included. 'Good morning, I'm Shelby Carter from Xerox, and I'm here to demonstrate this fine equipment.' We went through everything. 'You don't push the button. You touch it! You excite the paper. You don't start-it-up—crank-it-up. You ignite the machine.'

"Well, we went through the product, the people, the price and the customer elements. 'Good afternoon, Mr. Smith. Thank you for your business. And, by the way, I'd like some more.' We reindoctrinated our people on how to operate the equipment. I mean, to *really* understand it. When we say, 'Management by Example,' we expect to see our branch managers and general managers out in the field making calls.

"We'll have a particular theme for a certain period of time, and then we'll change to another one. One year our theme was 'Excellence in Management,' and in '76 it was 'Excellence in Execution.' We had signs all over the place at every branch office reading, 'Excellence in Execution.' Then we went to the theme

'Excellence in '77.' I believe that these themes help set a standard.

"You'll see us put an emphasis on the word 'excellence.'" Shelby smiles. "Again, it's a matter of pride for a person to strive to achieve excellence in whatever he does. One of my favorite quotes is by John Gardner. In his book *Excellence* he said, 'The society which scorns excellence in plumbing, because plumbing is a humble activity, and tolerates shoddiness in philosophy, because it is an exalted activity, will have neither good plumbing nor good philosophy. Neither its pipes nor its theories will hold water.'

"You like that one? Well, here's one of my original quotes: 'The pursuit of excellence in the face of adversity is invariably matched by the glory of the result.'

"Of course, when you speak about excellence, you have to relate it to the customer. The one expense we cannot afford is an unhappy customer. We're out there selling a service; it's not hardware we're selling. And in our case, it happens to be a finished copy. Back in my early days, I was selling electric typewriters, but it wasn't the equipment itself that I was selling. Instead, I was selling what that equipment would do. In those days, it was the electric typewriters versus manual ones. I'd tell a customer, 'The manual one requires your secretary to press the keys a quarter of an inch, but with the electric it's only an eighth of an inch. And the difference in that savings to your secretary in an average year is equivalent to her walking on her fingers from Baltimore, Maryland, to Columbus, Ohio, versus from Baltimore to California! What do you want her to do? Use a manual which takes two to three pounds of energy, or an electric which uses only a few ounces? The weight depression could be the difference between shoveling twenty tons of coal a day versus only five pounds. Now that's a tremendous savings of energy, isn't it?' I don't care what product a person is selling. If he can relate his product in terms of what it can do for his customer, he's performing a genuine service.

"When we were at our Corporate Training Center in Leesburg,

we conducted a course called 'Professional Selling Skills.' Part of it involves a questioning technique which puts the emphasis on listening. We'd ask questions such as 'What are your copying needs? Is time an important factor? Is copy quality the key? Is turnaround what you're after? Is it convenience for operators? Are you centralized? Do you make reports? Do you need reduction? Do you need two-sided copies? You see, we have to really dig into the customer in order to find out how we can provide him with a service. For example, the two-sided copying may be a factor because of the high cost of office space today, since it will reduce filing space requirements. And, incidentally, two-sided copying becomes a factor due to today's awareness of ecology. People are very interested in incorporating ways to save our nation's natural resources.''

Although Xerox has been the leader in the xerography field, the company has been sharing some of its patents and technological information with other companies which have sought and obtained Xerox licenses. So, rather than patents, it is manufacturing and marketing expertise that make for the company's success. It is significant that Xerox's net income and revenues for the three and six months ending June 30, 1977, were the highest of any quarter or half-year in the company's history up to that time. As Shelby puts it, "It really gets down to total customer service. And this is the real strength with Xerox or, for that matter, any company. It's providing the right product and service, coupled with the right administrative services.

"People have come to realize that Xerox is a reliable company," Shelby stresses. "We have a broad spectrum of products that will do anything the customer needs in the way of reproduction, and we give full service to the customer.

"I'll give you a fine example of how a very small, seemingly insignificant thing once influenced me when I was the customer. When our family had just moved into our new home—the whole gang: our six children and two dogs—it was the first day in the house and everything was in an uproar. The kids all poured into the family room, and the television set didn't work. I got out the Yellow Pages and called for a repairman, and he came right out. Well, after he repaired the set, he asked me to come over and look at it. I stepped over the kids, our German shepherd, the books, and instead of handing me a bill, he took out a bottle of Windex spray and cleaned the glass. That impressed me, because he showed me how proud he was of his work and the product he serviced. From that day on, whenever we've needed our TV fixed, I've said to my wife, 'Honey, call the Windex guy.' He's got pride in his work, and I respect him for that.

"This attitude of pride in your product gives the customer a sense of continuity and stability. He knows you care about your work and that you'll be back again. I think that the technique of not pushing a button, but touching it lightly, shows that you treat that machine with respect. And that's because you have pride in what you're selling.

"I believe it's very important for a company to thoroughly educate a salesperson so he or she fully understands the product," Shelby states. "When the sales reps *really* know the quality of the product, they're bound to develop pride, because they *believe* in it. Then, too, the company has to train them on salesmanship. It's not something a person's born with. He or she has to be taught how to sell. For example, unless a salesperson is taught how to close a sale, they may never know how to properly do it. As a result, most of them are weak closers. They get very meek when it's time to close. At Xerox, we tell them to start asking for the order, and to get the order blank out on the table as quickly as they can, so when it does come out, it's not a surprise. It's one of the first things I do when I'm making a presentation. I have all the material (the order pad and the pencil) lying right on the table.

"We also teach our salespeople how to make a trial close: 'Since all of the things which we just discussed are agreeable, sir, would you like to order the machine? Which color? Which one? Do you find this a necessary service?' If he replies no, I'll ask,

'Why not?' Then, you assume the sale by asking him to sign the order by saying, 'Press hard; there are five copies.' "

Shelby sits back, lets out a big laugh, and adds, "Actually, I should have told him to sign once, and we'd make four copies!"

He leans forward and continues earnestly. "I believe that when salespeople are properly trained to sell your product, they are going to have that required self-confidence to do a big job. There will be an inner pride because they know that they are good! You know, salesmanship is like the orchestration of a large symphony. You have all these different pieces, and you have to have them all working at the same time. You've got to get your whole act together.

"The point is, I want that sales rep to be fully equipped to handle any situation. You know, every now and then a green sales rep will ask me, 'Mr. Carter, I never know whether or not I should have a drink at lunchtime with a customer. What do you think?' My reply is, 'If you're going to drink at lunch, drink whiskey, not vodka. So your customers will know you've been drinking, that you're not stupid.' "

With a grin Shelby adds, "How in the world is that sales rep going to establish a confidence level with his other calls that afternoon if he's been drinking at lunch?"

Part of Shelby's huge success in sales management can be attributed to his pulling-no-punches attitude with his sales force. He has a way of getting right to the point, and the sales reps respect him for it. If, for example, he's trying to hammer home the message that a certain situation requires some selling creativity, he might quote Winston Churchill, "If there is no wind, row." Or he might use one of his favorite original quotes, "Toughness is the unswerving dedication to a principle, guided by the truth."

According to a recent *Money Magazine* article, executive recruiters in the United States rate Xerox among the ten best employers. Unquestionably, having someone like Shelby Carter head up the field operations for sales, service, and administration of all products sold in the United States has a lot to do with it. He's a top sales executive who thrives on going into the field to encourage his people by letting them know he understands how tough it is.

"Nothing happens until a sale is made," he will tell them. "Sure, I know it can be argued that nothing happens until you manufacture a product, but I say, 'Production minus sales equals scrap.' You may have a lot of production and a lot in the warehouse, but if you can't sell 'em, well, that's my definition of scrap!"

He may quote the famous Spanish bullfighter Domingo Ortega: "Bullfight critics ranked in rows/Crowd the enormous plaza full;/But only one is there who knows,/And he's the man who fights the bull." And then he adds, "This old picador from Rochester never forgets that you're the ones who have to fight the bull."

Shelby also interlaces his speeches with quotations from Shakespeare. "For the battle that the business world is today," he might say, "and it is a battle, you know, I'll pass on some words from Shakespeare's *Henry V*. The king told his troops before the Battle of Agincourt, 'And gentlemen in England now abed/Shall think themselves accursed they were not here.'"

And Shelby's people, observing the pride he takes in his company and what it stands for, are themselves imbued with that same pride.

6

Rich Port

(REALTOR)

"The key to success . . . is service."

Rich Port is chairman of the board of Rich Port, Realtor,®* one of the nation's larger real estate firms specializing in residential properties. Its estimated sales volume for the fiscal year ending December 31, 1978, will exceed $300 million.

Rich is also the chairman of the board of Nationwide Find-A-Home Service, Inc. He is a past president of the National Association of Realtors, the largest professional trade association in America, which has an estimated 600,000 membership. He served as president of the American Chapter-International Real Estate Federation; as president of the Illinois Association of Realtors; as president of the La Grange Board of Realtors; as president of the Realtors Computer Service, Inc.; and is a past chairman of the Marketing Management Council of the Realtors National Marketing Institute. Also, Rich is the dean emeritus of the Realtors Institute of Illinois; president of Rich Port Appraisal Corporation; president of Rich Port Development Corporation; a past president of the Midwest Chapter–Certified Residential Brokers; vice president of Dewey Insurance Agency; member of the American Management Association; member of the Chicago Association of Commerce & Industry; member of the Executive Club

*REALTOR® is a registered collective membership mark which may be used only by real estate professionals who are members of the National Association of Realtors and subscribe to its strict Code of Ethics.

of Chicago; a member of the Realty Club of Chicago; and a director of the First National Bank of Western Springs.

Rich's civic and community activities include: past lieutenant governor Kiwanis International; member of the board of trustees of the Lincoln Academy of Illinois; past president of the Kiwanis Club of La Grange; and past president of the West Suburban Chamber of Commerce. Rich has also served as chairman of the board and as a director for twenty years of the West Suburban YMCA; commander of the Robert E. Coulter, Jr., Post 1941, the American Legion; general chairman of the United Fund; commander of the Military and Hospitaler Order of St. Lazarus; division chairman of the Salvation Army and Chicago Metropolitan Area Executive Committee; state central committeeman of the Illinois Republican State Central Committee; associate board member of the Community Memorial General Hospital; assistant director of the La Grange Civil Defense; commander of the Chicago Chapter, Military Order of the World Wars; unit crusade chairman of the American Cancer Society; delegate to the Republican National Convention, 1976; life member of the National Guard Association of the U.S.; life member of the Reserve Officers Association of the U.S.; life member of the University of Illinois Alumni Association. He is also a member of the Illini Club of Chicago and the Zeta Psi Fraternity Alumni Association.

Rich is a life governor of the Realtors National Marketing Institute. In 1964 he was named the Illinois Realtor of the Year. The Illinois Association of Realtors also awarded him the Public Relations Award. He has received five first place awards, thirty-two citations, and six awards from the Realtors National Marketing Institute for business ideas. The American Salesmasters presented him with the Oscar of Salesmanship Award. The National Association of Realtors awarded him the Five-Diamond Pin Membership Award. Rich holds four professional designations from real estate institutes and societies and is a member of the International Real Estate Fraternity Lambda Alpha.

The Kiwanis International presented him with the Legion of Honor Award. In 1965 the West Suburban YMCA awarded him the Service to Youth Award, and in 1961 they presented him with their Special Award. He is a recipient of a Life Member Award from the American Legion. In 1976, he received the Alma Mater Award from St. Norbert College.

Rich was born on September 17, 1917, in Chicago, Illinois. He attended Western Military Academy, the University of Illinois, and St. Norbert College. He holds a B.S. degree.

Prior to forming Rich Port, Realtor, Rich spent six years in the real estate field as a salesman and a broker. He served in the European Theater during World War II and attained the rank of lieutenant colonel in the Infantry. In 1977 he retired from the Reserves as a brigadier general.

Rich and his wife, Mary Elizabeth, live in La Grange Park, Illinois. Mary is a Realtor and serves as treasurer of Rich Port, Realtor. Their daughter, Elizabeth Anne, is married to John Hallahan, who is the executive vice president of Rich Port, Realtor. The Ports have two granddaughters, Catherine Elizabeth and Patricia Leigh.

RICH PORT

"We're in a unique business," Rich Port explains. "In most other fields, a salesperson can offer his customer a product which will have some differences from his competitors'. But when we sell a residential property, we're often selling the same product which the buyer can purchase from the real estate office down the street. So in order for us to offer something better, we must give them more service. The key to success in the real estate business is service."

Rich Port has built one of the most successful real estate operations in the United States with this philosophy. Rich is chairman of the board of Rich Port, Realtor, an ever expanding firm with twenty-eight offices servicing the Greater Chicago Area, a 375-person sales force, and sales in excess of $300 million a year. Apparently this *serving the client* formula has worked very well for his organization.

Six feet tall and 245 pounds, Rich looks as though he might have played linebacker for the Chicago Bears during his younger days. His appearance and deep, commanding voice hardly seem the source to tell you, "We never use the word 'house' when we discuss residential property; instead, we say 'home.' You know, the word 'home' is the second most emotional word in the English language, next to 'mother.'"

And as you listen to him speak, you also notice that he seldom uses the word "I" but rather says "we." And although, by his own confession, he's a fierce competitor ("I hate to lose at anything, even a game of cards"), Rich Port is 100 percent committed to serving his client. Only after the client is satisfied will Rich think of his own interests.

"Sure, we're interested in the bottom line," he asserts. "What business isn't? But if one thinks in terms of his client first, everything else falls into place, and at the same time you'll make a profit, too. When we first began to sell multiple listings,* one of our salesmen didn't relish the idea of not getting the 100 percent commission, which he was accustomed to receiving on an exclusive listing. Well, every time he had a prospective buyer, he'd only show our homes. It was fine to show our homes, but while he was doing it, someone else might sell his buyer one of their listings. It happened to this salesman three times in a single month, and that was the end of that. He thought his people were so loyal to him they would only buy from him. It's his duty and obligation as a professional real estate person to find the right home for his buyers regardless of the amount of the fee."

Rich began his career in real estate in 1946 after spending more than seven years in the U.S. Infantry, becoming a lieutenant colonel. "When I returned after World War Two," explains Rich, "I did a lot of job hunting. It was a new experience for me, because I had never really worked at a civilian job. When interviewed, it was always two questions: 'What have you done?' and 'What can you do?' There was little to claim except a few military accomplishments and a college degree. At age twenty-eight I had no other real experience, and the jobs available to people with my qualifications weren't paying very much money. There were few openings for knife fighters and bayonet instructors. One evening I explained to a friend the disenchantment and frustration in my civilian life and asked for his advice. He told me I had a

---

*"Multiple listings" refers to a system whereby a property listed by one real estate firm can be sold by another, with the profits split fifty-fifty.

'super sales personality' and should go into selling and to be sure to sell something big! 'If you sell something big,' he said, 'you can make real money in selling. If it's not big, well, it's like the nose on your face . . . everybody has one.'

"After a sleepless night," Rich says, "about the biggest things I could think of were locomotives, which were made right in La Grange. When the plant opened that morning, I was the first one there. The personnel director explained they didn't need help to sell locomotives. They were so far behind in their orders there wasn't a need for salesmen. I tried other companies and found similar production problems. Finally it dawned on me: to sell real estate! After I'd read every book in the library on the subject of real estate, a local broker agreed to sponsor me for my licensing exam, which I passed. Again the real estate people asked me, 'What have you done? . . . What can you do?' This time I had a third item in addition to the Army experience and a college degree; a real estate broker's license could be added. Well, I was completely deflated when they asked me if I had ever sold anything, and my reply ended some interviews. Finally somebody put me aboard as his only salesperson.

"During the first eight months I earned our family's living expenses for the year," Rich continues. "However, in the ninth and tenth months, I sold nothing and almost left the business. I discussed the situation with my boss, and his only reply was 'It's a strange business.' In fact, any time I had a problem, he had one pat answer: 'It's a strange business.' Well, during the last two months of this first year, I had three sales in November and four in December, and realized real estate was where I belonged. And it's been very good to me ever since.

"It was total frustration that got me started in business for myself. I couldn't get my broker to move as fast as I thought he should. As an example, when I went to a door and said, 'My name is Rich Port from Roger Pratt's office,' and they would ask, 'Whose office?' That convinced me of one thing: If I were ever in business for myself, nobody would ever represent us and be asked, 'Who's Rich Port?' And I surely wouldn't tell a salesman with a problem that 'It's a strange business.' There had to be a better solution.''

Rich leans back in his chair and ponders. "I did a lot of thinking about how I would develop our image in the business. We were living in the Township of Lyons, and I thought, What if a life insurance agent represented the Lyons Township Farmers Mutual Life Insurance Company, and he was competing against a company such as Prudential or Travelers? Well, he'd have to make absolutely certain that his firm had a reputation for doing what it holds out to the public it's capable of doing. This was part of the image of the real estate business that I wanted to project to the community. An effective and continuous public relations program was absolutely essential to assure our success.

"Then I approached a local Realtor who was old enough to be my father," Rich explains. "We worked out an arrangement to be fifty-fifty partners in a business. He agreed to run the administrative functions of the office, and I'd be in charge of the sales organization. He was a fine gentleman, but again this grew into a frustrating experience because I wanted to move faster and believed we could make 500 percent more money, whereas he was delighted to continue producing the same income. He didn't want to gamble, and at his age the risk-reward ratio didn't warrant the expansion I craved. I believed I could do better on my own. He told me I'd never do more than I was doing with him. As it turned out, however, I made three times as much money my first year on my own.

"In the six years I had been in the real estate business, I accumulated $33,000, with which we opened our new office," Rich recalls. "We started on April 19, 1952, and by the end of the year we were down to the last $1,000. Everything went into creating the right image: the finest furniture, the biggest ads, the public relations effort—the whole works. We had the biggest show in town going, but we were doing less business than anyone could imagine. It didn't appear that way, but those were the facts. To tell the truth, we were at the point where we would have had to dissolve the business if things didn't materialize in the first quarter of 1953. As it turned out, it was a fabulous year.

"In the first nine months, we built the organization. We had six well-trained salesmen, and from January 1, 1953, we really began to obtain results. At this time a staff of six was considered a large suburban office."

In spite of some early warnings from the old pros in the real estate business, Rich Port, Realtor, had little turnover of salespersons. "In the beginning we decided to have the most highly educated, most professional salespeople in the community," Rich states. "Once, after I'd delivered a speech to our real estate board about my thoughts on training and developing new people, the old-timers told me I was crazy. They said I would make salespeople too smart for their own good. You see, I wanted to educate them so they could take a transaction from the listing right through the closing without any help from anyone. We wanted a truly professionally trained all-broker staff. Well, the old-timers believed if we made all of our people professionals, then they would open their own offices right down the street.

"What they were telling me is that I should keep my people dumb. Our people, meeting the public, representing our firm, and yet they should be dumb, so they won't go into business for themselves. Well, that kind of thinking made me furious. We felt if we couldn't make our operation so appealing to the staff, convincing them they were better off with us than in their own shop, well then there would have to be something wrong with the operation. In any event, if they left, we would be sure to help them succeed and continue to be friends.

"It was this kind of philosophy on which we built our business"—Rich beams—"and I want you to know that the current sales manager of our La Grange office was part of that first group. So was our assistant manager in the commercial investment division. And the managers of our La Grange Park and Western Springs offices also were of the original six men in our organization. The other two have retired and are living in Florida."

Rich comes from a family of professional people. His father was a physician. Other relatives were lawyers, doctors, and engineers. Growing up in this professional atmosphere probably had a lot to do with Rich's early desire to put major emphasis on having a professional real estate organization. Rich readily admits, "I was determined to be a professional and accumulate all the knowledge available. A professional person must always limit the claim of his ability to that which he is qualified to do."

Since the very beginning of his career, Rich has stressed developing people who eventually would take the same approach to the real estate business. Each month all the new salespersons participate in a training program conducted at the home office of Rich Port, Realtor, in La Grange. "There isn't any way a Realtor-Associate can properly function," Rich insists, "if he or she doesn't have a finger right on the pulse of the market. As an example, he has to know where to recommend his client go for financing, and that requires understanding what the current lending policies are of all savings institutions and whoever else happens to be in the mortgage business in the community. Of course, he has to be familiar with current FHA and VA financing policies. So you see, knowing the whole spectrum of financing is just one single, but very important, aspect of this business.

"Sure, we're going to teach our salespeople the basics of the business," Rich explains, "such as how many square feet are in an acre. And they'll learn about footings, heating and air-conditioning systems, and all those things which make up a home. But that's not the total education. We're going to teach them how to understand people and, most important, to recognize a buyer's needs. The salesman is a problem solver, so he has to be capable of determining the buyer's problems. But in order to do that, he must understand their requirements. For example, a client may be transferred. Or perhaps the client's present home is a two bedroom and they now have four children. In order to really help the client, the salesman has to *listen*. Not only is it a matter of listening to what the man and wife are saying, but listening to *what they really mean,* because they don't necessarily always say what they mean! So what it all boils down to is being a student of human behavior, knowing and understanding people.

"In our training program we cover virtually every facet of real estate as well as the general field of selling," Rich continues. "We have sales meetings on subjects such as 'Time Utilization,' 'Body Language,' 'Empathy with the Client,' 'Self-Motivation,' 'Self-Discipline,' 'Setting Goals: Both Short-Term and Long-Term,' 'How Properly to Show a Home,' 'Selling Sellers Successfully,' 'Closing a Sale'—you just name it, and we've taught it at one of our meetings. We believe strongly in role playing as a teaching technique, using video tape. Also, drilling in the sales skills is essential to success. This is best done at meetings in our local offices. Twice a month we conduct regional sales meetings with the combined sales forces of several of our offices attending. Then we have our general sales meetings for the entire Rich Port, Realtor, organization. Of course, it takes a large facility to accommodate everybody, so we conduct these meetings out-of-house. Usually a guest speaker is invited to these general meetings, and we have arranged for guest speakers from all over the country—Los Angeles, New Orleans, Denver, just to name a few."

Rich emphasizes that a real estate salesperson should participate in community affairs. "One of my strongest beliefs is that if an individual is going to partake of the community, he should take part *in* the community. And it's the job of everybody in the real estate business to continually try to make his or her community a better place to live. When the salesperson does this, he is *improving* the product. He's making it a better place to live today than it was yesterday. This improvement gives the salesperson this year's model to sell instead of last year's."

Rich Port is a leader who believes in leading by example. "It's hard to expect your people to become involved in the community unless you do. Although we never formally demand that our people participate, our new associates do participate when they see the example that the older members set with their community involvement." Rich Port is one of the most respected men in the

Greater Chicago Area for his dedication to civic and charitable activities. He has been the recipient of many awards and honors throughout his career; only a condensed version of this involvement has been recounted in the biography at the beginning of this chapter.

Rich's idea of service extends beyond the real estate business. A bronze tablet honoring him recently placed on the wall of Chicago's West Suburban YMCA lobby concludes: *Rich Port's dedicated and dynamic patriotism, community involvement, and philanthropic leadership stand as an example of volunteer service so vital to the retention of our American way of life.*

"We believe that our people should belong to the community in every aspect," Rich states. "Another thing, we believe that a real estate office cannot properly function if it is too far from the area it aims to serve. The magic distance is unknown, but beyond a certain point, your effectiveness falls off tremendously. For example, we have offices in La Grange, La Grange Park, and right next door in Western Springs. All are adjoining suburban villages located on the Burlington Northern commuter line to downtown Chicago. Each small village has its own personality, and local people like to work with local people."

Rich doesn't use the word "branch" when referring to such offices. "We don't want to create the image of a big impersonal corporation with its little local branch office in town," he explains.

"Everything we do is structured to provide service," Rich stresses. "That's the name of the game. An excellent example of what the word 'service' means in the real estate business is exemplified by June Hofmann. She is continually one of our top salespersons and now manages our Clarendon Hills office. June has been with us for twenty-three years and has always done business only on a referral basis. We believe she could do business on top of the water tower in Western Springs because people would seek her out. I remember one instance when she sold a home, and the buyer was so pleased that he sent her seven referrals, and one of them sent her nine more.

"Often June will get a call from one of her satisfied buyers (now friends) who will say, 'June, an acquaintance of mine has been transferred from Cincinnati, and I wonder if you and John could come over for cocktails and dinner tomorrow evening.' June and John go to the home, but before they even walk in the door, that Cincinnati couple has been sold on living in Western Springs. The host has also extolled June's qualifications and virtues for being able to put things together, and the couple was told that there's no firm finer than Rich Port, Realtor. After a few minutes of chatting with the man and wife, June has a complete picture of what they want to buy. In many cases, she will conduct only one or two showing presentations, and there won't be much she can do to keep those people from buying the property. That's because she's analyzed their needs so well and knows exactly how to match the benefits.

"Do you want to know June's secret?" Rich beams with pride. "*She kills her clients with service!* I mean it; she'll kill them with service, even *after they have purchased the home*. For example, she'll see to it that their water is turned on. If it requires a deposit because it has been turned off by the previous owner, she will make a deposit. She'll arrange to have the telephone installed. June knows all the answers including exactly what the student-teacher ratio is in each grade of the school, and she often calls the teachers by name. She tells people exactly—to the penny—how much it costs to get a monthly ticket on the suburban train. 'It's only nineteen air-conditioned minutes on the fastest train,' she may inform a buyer. June will have a gift for the family which may be in the home before they move in. The first day in the home she'll cater a meal. Or, knowing how inconvenient moving can be, she'll invite them to her home for dinner that first evening. She'll make sure that they are in the Newcomers' Club. June will call a church of their denomination and say, 'You have new possible parishioners, and you ought to meet them.' You name it," Rich boasts, "and June will do it. June helps the family adjust to the community in every way possible.

"Of course, this is the kind of person she is. She's the type who will bake a loaf of bread and bring it to a neighbor. June does it with sincerity and friendliness. She likes to serve, and that's why she never has time to accept business except by referral. As I mentioned, they seek her out. It's a privilege for a buyer to be fortunate enough to do business with her. A successful salesperson will provide so much service that the home seeker will be ashamed to do business with anyone else.

"My definition of a truly professional person in the real estate field," Rich proclaims, "is the individual who will not take opportunity time. By 'opportunity time' we mean the time a salesperson will spend 'on the floor' or, in our business, in the office to receive buyers who walk in or telephone calls from somebody who wants to either buy or sell real property. When a salesman works on a referral basis, it is estimated he'll sell perhaps two out of three referrals. On the other hand, the salesman who depends on getting his buyers initially from *For Sale* signs, advertising, walk-ins, and telephone calls will have a closing ratio of perhaps one out of ten or possibly twenty."

Rich believes that the true pro will have four things going for him when he's working with a referral. "The first is that the buyer is already sold on the salesman. Of course, that's due to third-party selling effort. Second, the potential buyer is convinced that the real estate firm is fully qualified to service him. Third, the couple has definitely decided on the community where they wish to live. Fourth, they must be sold on the product, which is, of course, the actual home. Now if it's the right kind of referral, somebody has said to this buyer, 'You can't do business unless you talk to June Hofmann. She's associated with Rich Port, Realtor, and there's no finer real estate corporation in Chicagoland. Now the place to live is Western Springs. We live there, and my parents raised our family there, and that's the place to live.' Well, when that buyer comes in, all the salesman has to do is to fit the needs of the buyer with the benefits of the property. If the salesperson will listen and observe the reactions, it's easy to put the sale together.

"It is not possible to emphasize too strongly how important it is for that salesman to listen to his buyer,'' Rich continues. ''Often what he says and what he means may be two entirely different things. Don't forget, buying a home is an emotional process, so people don't always say what they mean. The salesman has to listen very carefully. He must also realize that he is not going to be able to satisfy a buyer's needs 100 percent, so he must attempt to put it all together in the best possible way by matching the home with the buyer's requirements and what is realistic. After a salesman has shown a property, he should immediately sit down with the man and wife and ask, 'Well, tell me, how close have we come?' If he has a good working relationship with them, they will tell him. 'Really, we want a larger family room, a bigger back yard or to be closer to the school.' After he's worked with them for a little while, either the salesman will understand the problem, knowing the needs and requirements of the buyers, or it's a poor working relationship and they'll probably try someone else.

''Years ago,'' Rich reminisces, ''Mary and I decided that we wanted a cottage on a Wisconsin lake. We talked with a real estate salesman and told him we didn't want many steps from the cottage down to the water. It was very important to have flat ground. Also, we wanted a nice porch. We needed a place to relax and unwind, and a porch was very important to us. Well, you wouldn't believe it, but the first property he showed us had sixty-three steps going down to the lake and no porch! He showed us a couple of others, and they were no better. We weren't being fussy. We didn't care if it had two bedrooms or six bedrooms, and a family room wasn't an issue. We just wanted that porch and no steps. I told him, 'Charley, you're a great guy, and I like you, but you're not showing us what we want to buy. You don't understand what I'm saying, so let's go over it one more time.'

''To tell you the truth,'' Rich sighs, ''if I hadn't been in the business . . . The typical buyer would have sworn, 'This dumb so-and-so doesn't know what the hell he's doing. Let's go to someone else.' Anyway, the salesman has to qualify that buyer's requirements. He should listen attentively and write them down, and after he shows the property he might ask, 'How close did we come?' Again he should realize that he's never going to completely satisfy the client's pocketbook and also come up with the perfect home. There's bound to be some concessions.

"A salesman should feel a tremendous amount of satisfaction from assisting a family to find a home. Then, and only then, is he a true real estate salesman, in my opinion. But, I repeat, that salesman must have a complete desire to make that couple happy. It should be a thrill to him to know that he solved their problem about where they were going to live, raise their family, and give the children a good education.

"Of course, it's not always simple for the man and wife to make a decision, particularly after they've looked at a number of homes. So finally the salesman might sit down with them and put everything on paper listing the pluses and minuses of the homes under consideration. He might say, 'Now didn't you like the family room of this home? In your opinion isn't the back yard just the kind you want? Now over here I've itemized the advantages of this home. Here is a list of its benefits.' I think it's important to guide them, but to a degree you have to let the home sell itself. You must be careful not to apply any selling pressure. That's a dangerous and needless thing to do when selling a home."

After a brief pause Rich adds, "There will be times when you listen carefully to what a couple say they want, and you'll have the perfect property for them. Well, usually you should show them more than one home, so that they do have a choice. A choice of one is really not a choice at all, is it? They may surprise you by buying the other home instead of the one you had expected them to buy."

A warm smile appears on Rich's face, and he says, "So far I have only talked about the buyer, but the professional listing of real property for sale is the real estate business. In the beginning of my career it took me a couple of years to realize this fact. The salesman who establishes the proper relationship with his client, the seller, will discover that, in essence, it's the finest relationship that exists in the business world. You should consider it a partnership. A salesman should endeavor to understand exactly what his seller desires. Of course, his client wants to sell his home at the highest price and possibly in the shortest period of time. Well, the salesman's goal has to be the same as his client's. Both of them have to work out the best way to accomplish that goal. The salesman and the seller must work together, and it requires cooperation on the part of the homeowner. He has to be willing to have the home shown at times when it might not be too convenient. The wife will have to be ready to present the home to its best advantage quickly. Perhaps it will require the moving of a baby grand piano out of a small living room, or replacing a dead bush on the front lawn or adding some touch-up paint to the exterior of the home. And it's important for the seller to cooperate and allow a *For Sale* sign to be placed in front of the home, because in most areas 10 to 19 percent of the buyers are produced from this source.

"It must be a joint effort on the part of the seller and the salesman, and the salesman has to convince the seller to establish a realistic price and not utilize the 'price cure' system. In the price cure system, the property is placed on the market at an exorbitant price, and gradually, over a period of time, the seller becomes convinced that his price was too high, and he gradually lowers it until it finally reaches the marketplace. To be quite frank, then and only then is it worthwhile for the salesman to spend his time trying to market the property. A salesman will go hungry if he works on overpriced property. So the whole key in this business is to think in terms of the best interest of the seller, the buyer, and the real estate salesperson by pricing properties as realistically as possible.

"The method we use at Rich Port, Realtor, is to have a number of our people inspect the home and to have each of these individuals indicate their independent opinion of the market value. We then determine what we consider to be the four most comparable properties recently sold in the area. We must compare apples with apples and make plus and minus adjustments. Following that procedure, we make a cost approach to the value which normally establishes the upper limit of value. After that we qualify the home by asking eleven questions, of which we expect at least nine to be answered in the affirmative. We list all the features which we think are attractive, and we have another list for the things we believe are not as desirable about the property. Maybe it's too far from school, or perhaps it backs up to a gas station. Whatever the pluses and minuses are, we put them down on paper so we can understand them and plan our marketing approach. After this we analyze the information gathered and ask ourselves, 'Well, where do you think it's going to sell? What's the bottom price he will have to take for the home?' Well, say it's $55,000.

"Now what if 'Mr. Right' comes along? He's the buyer who likes everything about the property. The home has beige carpeting, and he loves beige carpeting. He likes photography, and the home has a darkroom. His father always had a pin oak tree in the back yard. He wants one. There *is* a pin oak tree in the back yard. His wife raises roses, and there's twenty-five blooming rose bushes in the front yard. What would Mr. Right be willing to pay for the property—$60,000? Perhaps we'll have to wait for two years for Mr. Right to come along, but the seller should be given a reasonable opportunity to find Mr. Right. Although we arrive at this figure of $57,500, this is a figure midway between the bottom price and what Mr. Right will pay. There's nothing wrong with a price of $60,900 or $61,500. It is traditional to price a home a little above top dollar estimates, because appraising is not an exact science."

Rich adds seriously, "One of the most difficult problems we have in pricing a home is that the seller will often be guided by emotions. He might have purchased the home guided by emotions, and now he attempts to justify it in his mind when he gets ready to sell. He sees his home as a mother looks at her children. You cannot convince a mother that her child is homely. Nor can you convince a seller that his home is the worst one in the block. The owners may be the least qualified persons in the world to establish the price.

"A friend could call me from Pittsburgh," Rich explains, "and tell me that his home has been on the market for X amount of time, and it hasn't sold. My first question to him would be 'Well, is your house unusual for your neighborhood?' If he says that it isn't, I would want to know if other similar homes in the area are selling. If he replies, 'Yes, one down the street just sold, and another one, and so on . . .' I can analyze the problem and say, 'Hey, your price is probably too high.' Some homeowners remind me of a man who runs into the doctor's office with a terrible pain in his side. After the doctor examines him, he announces, 'Your appendix is about to rupture and it must be removed immediately.' Well, the man says, 'That's a lot of bunk. I have measles.' In essence this is what the real estate person is up against occasionally with the emotional seller. The truly professional salesperson will convince him that it's important to price his home as realistically as possible, and it can't be done emotionally or illogically.

"In certain subdivisions where dozens of homes almost exactly like the client's have been sold, you could take the comparison book for that area, hand it to him and say, 'Here, look over the sales in the past sixty days, and you tell me what your home is worth.' The chances are that he could pin it down fairly close. It isn't any big mystery. The most recent sales are the best yardstick for measuring value.

"However, if the home hasn't moved within a couple of weeks, the professional does not call the seller and say, 'Perhaps the price is too high. You have to reduce the price.' If it was properly priced in the beginning, you should sell your product close to that price; it's as if you were buying a loaf of bread or a gallon of milk at the grocery store—you don't dicker and make the grocer an offer. You pay the price, and that's the way it would be in the real estate business if it were an exact science—but it isn't! There are too many amenities which make up value, and therefore there's a certain amount of estimating in determining the value. But when you get right down to it, the buyer is the one who's spending the money; so he's the one who decides what the actual price will be. He might say, 'I won't pay more than $56,500 for that home.' The man tells the seller our best offer is

$56,500. The seller may think for a moment or two and reply, 'I'm ready to go. Let me sign the contract.'

"Do you want to know what the real secret is in working with the seller? Once the salesman has the property on the market at a realistic figure, he has to keep in constant communication with the seller. Whenever you find a frustrated, disgruntled seller in the marketplace, it's because he hasn't been told what's taking place with the sale of his home. It's usually just plain bad communication! A client should never, and I repeat *never,* have to call the salesman to find out what's happening if he is properly doing his job. A professional Realtor-Associate is in constant contact with the seller. He'll call and tell him everything that's going on. 'We just received a mortgage commitment on your property this morning. We can get so many dollars for so many years.' Perhaps he'll call back on the same day and say, 'That buyer who looked at it yesterday, well, he probably isn't going to buy, but I have someone coming in tomorrow. I suggest that you keep the lights on in the living room, the ones on the end tables. Is eight P.M. OK for tonight?' If there's nothing to call about, then there is something wrong with the salesman—it means he is not doing anything. 'Today we submitted your home to the multiple listing service. Tomorrow a photographer is coming out to take a picture of the home.' Or another call might be 'Say, I just wrote this ad last night. Will you help me before I submit it to the newspapers? Let me read it to you. Also, a VA appraiser is coming out on Wednesday. He'll be there around three. Is that all right?' The secret is to keep in constant touch with the seller. Let him know what's happening. The typical real estate office does so much more to merchandise a piece of property than the seller knows about. And *that's because they don't tell them!* Of course, the salesman can do all of these things and keep it a secret, and he'll end up with a frustrated seller. The client will scream his head off, 'My home is still on the market. What a no-good bum this salesperson is.'

"The real professional will never have a disgruntled seller," Rich insists, "because he is always communicating. We tell the public that we're capable of merchandising their home. When we don't and a listing expires, we have really stumbled. The image of our corporation has become tarnished. That seller is unhappy, and he will tell his friends and neighbors about it. Realtors in general take a step backwards in their effort to achieve a professional approach. The entire industry is hurt because we failed to do the job. When you hold out to the public that you are capable of doing a job, and you don't do it, that's really damaging your reputation in the community. If you get a number of expired exclusive listings, it's similar to an attorney who loses too many cases in court. Or it's like the doctor who loses too many patients on the operating table. Soon the hospital chief of staff is going to say, 'Doctor, you know you're not really qualified, and we must limit your practice.' *You have to do what you hold out to the public that you are capable of doing!"*

Recently, Rich Port sent the following bulletin to all personnel at Rich Port, Realtor: "It is easy to classify some complaining clients as 'unreasonable.' On very rare occasions, it is probably justifiable to label some complaining clients as 'unreasonable;' however they are still clients. When we are totally professional in our approach to this business, we will know how to properly do business with all clients, including the unreasonable ones."

Currently Rich Port, Realtor, is selling 96 percent of its listings within the term of the listing agreement, usually 90 to 120 days. That's great when you consider that national statistics indicate the average is around 50 percent to 60 percent. "I've seen firms publish that they were very proud to have sold 65 percent of everything they listed," Rich grunts. "That means 35 percent of their clients died on the operating table. I surely would not want to put those figures in print!"

Rich claims that much of his firm's success in having an amazingly high closing-to-listings ratio is owing to the fact that they carefully evaluate every property prior to accepting it as a listing. "If somebody comes to you with a piece of property which he built out in the middle of the desert, you should think twice about listing it. Say the seller had unlimited wealth, and he put fourteen-carat gold doorknobs, marble baths, and a dozen fireplaces into the home. Doesn't matter! Because not many people want to live in the desert. The ideal price is based on what the typical buyers will pay—not on the value of brick and mortar. It's also what the buyers will pay during a normal exposure period in the marketplace. If the salesman knows that the property is too high priced, and the listing will probably expire due to the difficulty in selling it, and he's going to have an unhappy seller, he should turn down the job. Someone else may be better qualified to merchandise the home. It's a similar situation to the doctor who tells his patient, 'I'm not capable of doing this bypass surgery on your heart; you are going to have to see a specialist down in Houston, Texas.'

"Another good example is the man who recently paid $50,000 for his home and has put another $30,000 into improvements. Well, it's in a $50,000 block, and when he goes to sell it he's not going to be able to get $80,000 if the other homes are all still going for $50,000 at the time. Here again it is a matter of communication. The salesman must explain the home is overimproved, and he is not going to be able to realize the amount of money he has invested." Rich grins. "My own home is similar. We have spent a lot of money improving our property and now have the most expensive home on the block. Consequently, our home is not appreciating as much as it would if it were in a different location."

Many decisions of Rich Port, Realtor, are based on statistics which the firm has accumulated over many years. "Our statistics show," Rich explains, "that if a salesman works on properties which are priced 5 percent above fair market value, his time is currently worth perhaps sixty dollars per hour. If the property is priced 10 percent above fair market value, he is working for twenty dollars per hour. If the percentage goes to 15 to 20 percent above fair market value, he is working for six dollars per hour. In other words, his time can be worth as much as ten times more when he is working with a listing that has a realistic price. Time is the salesman's most precious commodity. Therefore, the manner in which he effectively economizes his time is vital to his total success.

"So many salesmen just don't know how to use their time to the best advantage, and it is my opinion that everything one does in business has to be properly related to the time that is required to get maximum results. The average real estate salesman will seldom spend two hours out of an eight-hour day having eyeball-to-eyeball contact with either buyer or seller. When you stop to figure that out, only 25 percent of any eight-hour day can result in producing income. that's why doctors are able to generate such high incomes. They have contact with patient after patient, with a reception room full of them waiting. As one patient is led out, the next one enters; and that goes on throughout much of the day. In the real estate business, and I suppose the same thing applies to most selling, the next customer may be some distance away. Perhaps the salesman has to pick up his buyer at the airport, and it takes an hour to drive back to the property. So there's a lot of legwork which goes on between presentations.

"For example, just a small thing like driving to work each morning can be properly utilized. We tell our people they should not come to work the same way every day. They should take different routes to find out what is going on in the area. They should look around to see if there is a new building that has just been erected, or perhaps a home has just been offered for sale. And there is nothing wrong with stopping to say hello to a friend who might be out in the front yard mowing the grass.

"I can recall coming to work one day, and a new salesman was sitting at his desk looking out the window. A few minutes later he was still staring out the window. I asked him what he was doing, and he replied, 'Nothing. There's nothing to do.' I said, 'In that case, you stay right where you are, and I'll be right back.' I came back a few minutes later with a list titled *24 Things to Do When You Think There Is Nothing to Do*. It must have worked, because he is still on our staff. Copies of that list are still given to our new salesmen today. The person who uses his time properly can accomplish anything. It upsets me to see a salesman sitting around discussing the weather, last night's ball game, the showing he had the other day, or knocking the competition. The professional always has more to do than he can possibly accomplish.''

Rich Port is a man who not only economizes his time on the job but who thoroughly enjoys working. ''I can remember some years ago when my Mary suggested I take Sundays off.'' Rich shrugs. ''One Sunday morning I said, ''Well, honey, what do I do now?' She suggested the hedge needed trimming, so I trimmed it and then I asked, 'Well, what now?' She suggested that I read the newspaper, so I did. Then I asked, 'What now?' Her answer? 'For heaven's sake, go to your old office.' So I took a shower, dressed, and was on my way. I was completely frustrated by not knowing what was going on in the office on a working day. I *had* to *be* there. I realize that there are people who successfully build a business some other way, but I didn't know how. My Mary has been of tremendous value in building our corporation. It takes a good cooperating wife, an understanding wife, a sacrificing wife to tolerate the working conditions and the frustrations associated with the real estate business. Also, extroverts with superegos plus the typical salesman's highs and lows are not easy to live with.

''Our offices are open seven days a week with the exception of the major holidays such as Christmas and Thanksgiving. But everyone has an office key and can go there at any time. One should remember that salespeople, normally, will seldom work any harder or longer than their sales manager.

''It is just as Vince Lombardi said, 'It's that extra effort, that total commitment.' Often I call many people in this business 'toe temperature testers.' They want the business . . . they go down to the shore, put a toe in the water to see if it is cold or warm, and check the wind. The truly ambitious individual is not a toe temperature tester. He jumps right in and gets wet all over. He goes the whole way. He puts it all together. He bakes the cake now with all the right ingredients. Most people know what these success ingredients are. They are just not willing to *pay the price* to be successful, that's all!''

There's not a thing, no matter how small, that Rich overlooks in his business. When he was personally selling real estate, he would never pull into a driveway with a potential buyer. "I would park down the street because it is so important that the buyer approach the home for the first time from the most advantageous view. You know, it is that first impression." He smiles. Rich always made it a point to jot down the names of the client's children and *even the dog's name!* "Let's say the dog's name was Sparks. Well, the next time I'd visit, I would call him by name. Boy, I'll tell you that when people are nice to my dog and call him by his right name, I like it." Another thing Rich did during his selling days was always to have an active list of four people seriously interested in the purchase of homes he had shown. "If I didn't have four hot potential buyers," he states, "I would start turning over rocks and beating the bushes to find buyers to inspect my listings. This is the best way to avoid having a slump."

When you enter a Rich Port, Realtor, office, you'll feel comfortable because of its relaxed, homey atmosphere. There's no steel furniture; each office is equipped with warm home-style furniture, and there will probably be a *Ladies' Home Journal* or a *Better Homes and Gardens* magazine on a coffee table. "The typical couple," Rich explains, "will first pick a particular suburb. Next they will plan a tour, perhaps drive through the neighborhood on a Sunday afternoon. Maybe the wife will talk to some of the people who live there, or they'll look in the newspapers. Many different things may happen before they finally get the courage to walk into a real estate office. They may be somewhat apprehensive about what's going to happen. I think that it is very important for the Realtor-Associate to put them at ease quickly. That's why we have the warm, friendly, homelike environment. We'll offer them coffee. If it is a cold winter night, in some of our offices there may be a crackling fire in the fireplace. During December, the Christmas tree will be lighted. The point is we think the people should feel right at home."

Rich is always on the lookout for new ideas. He won't hesitate to borrow one, perhaps refine it, and then *use* it. (One of these ideas, for example, came from a form letter he received from the president of an airline.) His prime motive is always to seek new ways to attract and better serve a client.

One of Rich's chief idea sources can be traced to his involvement in various real estate activities. Within the industry, Rich is one of the more active individuals in the United States, as witnessed by his almost unprecedented participation in local, statewide, and national associations (see the biography at the beginning of this chapter). "If I can get an idea from a car wash, just think what I can learn by exchanging ideas with the top people in real estate from all over the country," he jokes. Then he adds in a serious tone, "The real estate business has been so good to me that my association involvement also gives me an opportunity to pay back a small part of what I owe the business. As long as I can make a contribution, I will continue to remain active."

7

Edna Larsen

(AVON)

"A combination of work habits and self-discipline..."

Edna Larsen is considered the number one Avon Representative in terms of consistent customer service, a remarkable achievement, considering that there are approximately 975,000 active Representatives selling Avon products to customers in their homes in the United States and twenty foreign markets.

Edna began selling Avon in November 1958, when she and her family moved to North St. Paul, Minnesota, where they still live.

Like all Avon Representatives, she is an independent contractor, with a business of her own. While Avon Representatives generally sell in their spare time to earn extra income, Edna devotes long hours of regular and dedicated service to her long list of customers, whom she affectionately calls "my girls."

Over the years, Edna has received every achievement award offered by the company, including a dinette group, a stereo, a fur coat, and a trip to Hawaii.

Born in Parkers Prairie, Minnesota, she presently is Avon Representative for a large portion of North St. Paul, where her husband, Harold, is employed in maintenance by the North St. Paul School System.

The Larsens have three married daughters—Janice Nelson, Patricia Ciresi, and Katherine Larsen (whose husband happened to have the same family name)—and four grandchildren—Brent, Bradley, Beth, and Dawn. They live nearby, and give Edna a helping hand with shopping and other errands while she makes her Avon calls.

As an Avon Representative, housewife, mother, and grand-mother, Edna is a very busy woman. But she still manages to spend some time each day reading the Bible.

"I'm just an ordinary housewife," Edna Larsen insists. "I always tell my girls when Avon's offering a special, because I know how I like to save money, so I'm sure that they do too."

While Edna may feel she's an ordinary housewife, she certainly is no ordinary saleslady. She is considered a leading salesperson by Avon Products, Inc., a $1.4 billion corporation whose cosmetics, fragrances, and costume jewelry are sold by about 975,000 Representatives throughout the world. To rank tops among such an impressive number of independent direct salespersons qualifies her as an *extraordinary individual* indeed.

Edna began her sales career with Avon in November 1958, immediately upon moving from Carlos, Minnesota, to North St. Paul. "On our first day in our new home, we were in a state of mass confusion. As we unpacked, an Avon Representative knocked on the door," Edna recalls. "Well, she told me that my cousin had recommended me as a possible Representative because she felt sorry for me, since I was new in town and didn't know anybody. My cousin thought that I would get lonesome and bored, but by selling Avon I would get acquainted with everyone. Anyhow, that's how I got started, and I've been selling ever since."

Today, Edna's busy, hectic schedule can hardly be classified as boring. Edna has been running at 110 miles per hour ever since she began her Avon business. And she certainly isn't lonesome, as her cousin had feared she might be. "My husband, Harold, is the maintenance man at the North St. Paul school," she says, "so every kid in town knows him. They all love him, and everyone calls him Lars. Well, they've all seen me at their homes calling on their mothers and big sisters, so when Harold and I walk down the street in North St. Paul, a town of 12,000, we're like a couple of celebrities. Every kid will run up and give us a big hello.

"I can remember one time when Harold picked me up at one of my girls' homes, and a little boy saw me getting into the car. He got all excited and screamed to his mother, "Hey Mom, Lars is taking the Avon Lady away!""

Edna laughs and adds warmly, "I don't refer to them as customers. *They're my girls.* I want you to know that I love every one of them. They're just beautiful people. And I'm not just referring to their skin-deep beauty, thanks to my Avon products. I'm talking about what's underneath."

Like many women, Edna won't admit her age, but it's a surprise to be informed that she's the grandmother of two boys and two girls. She's obviously a living witness that Avon products do give good skin care. "I have friends tell me that my skin has really improved since I began selling Avon." She smiles. "I love to hear them tell me that. I want you to know that there's nothing but Avon in my house. I love the company and I love their products and I really believe in what I'm selling."

When she calls on her "girls," Edna offers an array of products for the whole family, attractively illustrated in a sales brochure. A new issue of the brochure is published for each two-week selling campaign, during which many products are featured at special reduced prices. The product line totals more than 600 individual items, considerably more than the original five fragrances with which founder David McConnell launched Avon in 1886. When various makeup shades and types of fragrances are included, the total more than doubles. The selection

EDNA LARSEN

includes makeup, skin care, fragrance, and bath products for women; men's cologne, talc, and aftershave; and grooming products for children and teenagers. In the beauty business, fashion and taste change constantly, and so does the Avon line to keep pace with trends. Often Avon introduces more products in a two-week campaign than other companies do in a year. With so many introductions, each time Edna visits her customers she has something fresh and exciting to show and tell them.

As another part of her sales philosophy, Edna also knows how important it is that a salesperson's physical appearance be just right. She believes that this is particularly true for a woman who sells cosmetics, especially one who visits her customers' homes. Her hair is impeccably groomed, and every last detail of her makeup is exact. Just the right amount of eye shadow and mascara. Not too much; just enough. "I believe that it's very important for me to dress properly and to wear my makeup well, but I don't overdo it," she explains. "While I always wear one of our fragrances, I never wear a strong one. You must think about how other people will react, and when you're visiting so many people's homes, you've got to realize that some of them may be sensitive, so you can't apply too much perfume."

When Edna calls on one of her customers, she always has a big smile on her face, and although they know she's a dedicated businesswoman, Edna is also their friend. "You have to take an interest in them," she stresses. "I can't just walk into some homes and get right down to business. I have to visit with them. Have a cup of coffee and relax them. I must be sure that they're at ease before I start selling. Just the other day, a lady told me, 'Edna, I'm sure you don't care to hear or see something new in our home, but nevertheless, you always take the time to look. And you always take time to make comments. You know, I really appreciate it.' Well, the fact is that *I do care*. I sincerely take a real interest in all of my girls. I listen to their problems. And if a housewife is bored and lonely, I'll stay a few extra minutes to keep her company."

Even though Edna has an exciting career and enjoys it

thoroughly, it takes an "extra something" to enable her to repeat her stupendous sales production week after week, month after month, year after year. Michelangelo once said something to the effect that , "If people knew how hard I worked to get my mastery, it wouldn't seem so wonderful at all." And if Edna's customers could spend a day with their Avon Representative, they'd see a different side of the Edna who appears to be so relaxed and at ease while she sips coffee and enthusiastically demonstrates her Avon products.

A typical day for Edna begins when she makes her first call at nine in the morning, and her day won't end until nine or ten that evening. "I'll make my morning calls until noon, and then I'll stop at home to grab a quick lunch which my husband will have waiting for me. Many times I'll eat in fifteen minutes, with a sandwich in one hand and the phone in the other while I'm frantically trying to set up appointments for the afternoon or evening. Nowadays, women are busy, and many of my girls want me to only work with them by appointment. They want me to call on them at their convenience, and, of course, I always do. When I first got started in this business, women weren't so active, so I was able to just stop by their houses, and they were always in. But times are different now.

"After lunch and my phone calls, I'm back out until five-thirty, and I come home again for a quick meal. My husband, God bless him, has the meal prepared, so I sit down to eat, and within a half hour I'm out for the evening. By the time I get home, which is normally between nine and ten every evening from Monday through Friday, I'll get into bed with a book and fall asleep with it. Sure there have been some evenings when I've been so tired that I practically collapsed as soon as I hit the bed, but when my alarm goes off the next morning, I'm ready to get started and literally jump out of bed. To tell you the truth, I can't wait to make my first call. Yes, I know there's a lot of salespersons who dread getting out of bed to make that first call, but I honestly love it. I can hardly wait to get going."

Edna pauses to collect her thoughts, then rapidly fires out,

"You know, this is my own business, so I don't have a boss. I can do whatever I want, whenever I want. There's no time clock to punch, so I don't have to be at an office or a plant at a certain time, and I don't have to stay on the job until the whistle blows to signify that it's the end of the day. I've got complete freedom to do as I please. But like any professional person, I place a high value on my time. Often a friend will ask me, 'Edna, why can't you go to lunch with me? *You're allowed!*' I have to explain that I work in this business exactly as if I do have a time clock to punch and a boss. And I have a tough boss at that—me!"

Edna is a highly disciplined person, and she won't allow any distractions to interfere with her workday. "My family has been very cooperative, and without them I couldn't possibly enjoy success in this business," she states. "I never, absolutely never, do an errand such as going to the supermarket, picking up the dry cleaning, or stopping at the drugstore when I should be selling Avon. I know many salespeople who waste an hour or two every day when they could be making calls. And they'll take an hour and a half for lunch every day, and then knock off early, say at four-thirty every day. What amazes me is that these same people wonder why they aren't earning enough money to make ends meet. Thank God, I've got Harold and my three wonderful daughters. They do all the shopping and errands that I would have to do if it weren't for them. And Harold does all my paperwork for me. So my time is freed up to be working full steam without any interruptions to distract me. You know, the way I look at it, I work as if I were paid by an employer, and if I goofed off I'd be in serious trouble.

"I once heard that the average salesperson spends less than 25 percent of his or her time eyeball-to-eyeball with a customer," Edna continues. "Well, I'm spending more than 90 percent of my time with customers, and I've got to think that's the only way an individual can make any money in sales.

"There's always an excuse a salesperson can have if he or she doesn't want to work. There's dozens of reasons why I *shouldn't* work if I didn't feel like it. For example, we get some of the coldest, harshest winters in the country. So I could always say the icy weather or a four-foot snowfall kept me from making my calls. Or I could have a cold or a headache like so many sales-people do, and stay home for a few days every now and then. Of course, there's always car trouble, too. Well, the fact is I don't let anything *ever* stop me.

"I remember one big snow we had," she continues. "We must have had close to four feet of snow on the ground. Well, finally it got so bad that I couldn't drive in it. So I parked my car, and I had to carry my sample cases and walk. The only other person who was doing much walking that day was the mailman, so I just walked in his tracks. My girls would greet me at the door with their heads shaking and say, 'Edna, I don't believe it! Only you could call on me in this weather. Come on right in.' Most outside salespeople don't work in bad weather, such as a big snowfall or a heavy rain, but I find that those can be my most productive days. Why? Because those are the days when you're going to find the most people at home. And they really appreciate you for calling on them. They know that they can count on you, and that's great for a salesperson's credibility.

"I practically live in my car," Edna continues. "So I keep it in tip-top shape and always buy a new one every two or three years. There's no excuse for a salesperson to miss work due to a non-operating car. Of course, sometimes it can't be avoided because you might be in the boonies and break down, but whenever I have trouble I just give my husband a call, and Harold drives right over and I use his car! He once said that it reminded him of the pony express."

Much of Edna's success stems from her strong emphasis on dependability. She believes that it's a salesperson's obligation to provide the customer with service, and she sees that her customers receive the finest service that she can humanly provide. Edna is so insistent that she perform her *duty* that her friends and family sometimes claim it's become a fetish. But Edna is quick to defend herself. "That's just the way I am. If I'm going to do something, I have to do it the best way I know how. Besides, I provide three

services, which is why my girls need me. First, I offer convenience, because I come to them rather than them going to a store
to shop. Second, Avon represents a savings because not only are
our prices very competitive, but our customers save money on
gasoline, parking, and, of course, particularly if they're working
girls, a dollar value can be placed on the time they save. And
third, I offer them personalized care, which is something that is
quite often missing in society today.

"I recently had a lady call and tell me that she was out of her
hormone cream and she wondered if I had any on hand. I told her
that I didn't, and she asked me if I minded if she went to a local
store, because she had to have some. I said that I didn't. After she
went downtown to one of our department stores with a large
cosmetic department, she called me back in disgust to report
about the poor service she received. 'Not only were the store
creams more expensive,' she said, 'but, Edna, you can't imagine
the abuse I had to take from the saleslady. I tried to ask her for
some information, and she would barely answer me. She kept
tapping her fingers on the counter, and looking at me as if she
was thinking, Hey, lady, there's nothing that's going to help you,
so just forget it. I told her that if she was going to give me that
kind of service, I was going back to my Avon lady.' "

A smile of satisfaction flashes on Edna's face. "My girls like
the personal care that I extend to them. I always have samples for
them to try, and I believe that they feel much more comfortable
trying them on in their homes than in a store. And I discuss each
item with them. I really try to educate them about our different
products, and I give them my personal comments on how they
look. I really think people appreciate that kind of service.

"So often I develop new customers from the daughters of my
old ones. As little girls they would sit in and listen to me talk with
their mothers about cosmetics, and as they become teenagers, I
begin to sell them merchandise, too. Today, teenagers are very
aware of their makeup, and because they have their own money
from babysitting and other jobs, they can be very big buyers. I'm
very careful, however, that I don't let them buy without their

mothers' permission. If I did, I would get a lot of mothers mad at me for overselling their daughters.''

Every two weeks Avon launches a new campaign with brochures featuring a number of different ''specials,'' products to be sold at tremendous savings. For an upcoming campaign, each Representative receives a package containing customer brochures and literature explaining the new products. ''I make sure that I read every single word of any material I receive from Avon,'' Edna declares. ''I know that some other salespeople don't do their homework like I do, but I read everything, and I study it to be sure that I can properly explain it to my girls. I believe that I'm much more effective with them when they see how informed I am about my products. I mean, I'd feel foolish just taking out a bunch of jars and bottles and not knowing what to say about them!''

Edna cuts no corner that could possibly short-change her customers. Although most other Avon Ladies carry only one sample case, she carries three. ''My husband and daughters keep telling me that I shouldn't carry anything so heavy.'' Edna sighs. ''Each one of those bags must weigh close to twenty-five pounds. But I feel that it's important to be able to show actual samples, and of course have some goodies for my girls to try during a demonstration Sure, it's extra work, but I believe it helps sell more Avon products. They want to touch and smell something before they buy it. While I don't have any actual information to back it up, I bet that I carry more sample bags than any other Avon Representative in the country.''

If one observes the Larsen household, it becomes obvious that it's an Avon home. In addition to the many plaques and awards Edna has received, the family has accumulated practically every decanter ever produced by the company. ''This one here is a collector's item,'' Edna proudly points out. ''The one over here is very valuable, too. And I wouldn't take $300 for the one on that table.

''So, as you can see, I definitely believe in what I'm selling,'' she boasts. ''I use Avon products only. I would never think of using anything else, but, of course, they're the best, so why should I? Now that doesn't mean I won't shop around at the local department stores and drugstores to find out what my competition is selling. I feel a salesperson develops confidence when he or she understands the competition. It's when you don't know what they've got that you're most likely to lack self-confidence and feel awkward with a customer. But by understanding my competition's products as well as my own, I can offer a real service. When a girl asks me, 'What should I use for my skin?' I can tell her. And I've got to be able to have the right answer. I don't care what a person's selling, he has got to know not only his product but also his competition's. If not, well, forget it!

"One of the greatest things for my confidence," she asserts, "was a trip to Avon's Morton Grove, Illinois, manufacturing laboratory. Several years ago, I had the privilege of visiting there to see how everything was made. Not only did I get an education about what I was selling, but I was amazed to see how 'hospital clean' the place was. I mean, you could eat off the floors! Well, I was really impressed, and it gave me added confidence in selling my products."

Although Edna works three territories instead of the usual one, she feels that she thoroughly understands each of her girls. (Incidentally, a typical Avon territory consists of approximately 200 homes.) "It's very important that you understand your customer," she claims. "Each one has to be treated somewhat differently, and I make it a point to handle them on an individual basis.

"For example, I have a notebook which lists the times when it is best to call on each girl. The busy ones like it when I get in and out real fast. And there are other girls who are eager to have me visit with them. While the average call will last approximately a half hour, some of the girls really like to talk, and if I'm not careful, I could be there all day. Like I said before, I've got to show that I'm interested in them, but I must also always be aware that I'm working. Therefore, I'll finally come right out and tell my long-winded girls that I'm working, and I must go. If a girl insists that I stay, and I find that she's continually making me stay much longer than I should, I will then have to make a decision as to whether I should even call on her in the future.

"I never want to stop calling on a girl, but if she doesn't let me out of the house, well, I might be faced with a situation where I'm losing money by making the call due to the great amount of time I spend with her. So I guess it's important to develop the technique of making a break from the customer, but at the same time being nice about it. Probably the best method to make the quick break is to use the old look-at-your-watch technique. That's when you glance at the time and convincingly announce, 'I've only got five minutes. I'm running late for an appointment. I'm sorry, but you must excuse me. I must be running.'"

A look of concern appears on Edna's face as she thoughtfully adds, "You can never have dollar signs showing in your eyes in this business. The girls have to know you're their friend, and they must know that you like them. You have to be able to joke with them, and to listen to their problems. I tell every new customer, 'I'm Edna to you. Please call me Edna.' And I tell every one of them, 'I want to be your friend.'

"I know all of my girls so well that I don't even have them sign the order pads." She smiles. "I wouldn't feel comfortable with some of them I've worked with for nearly twenty years if I had to ask for a signature to secure the order. You see, we've developed a very close relationship over the years."

Edna quickly emphasizes, "Another thing I believe an Avon Representative must be very careful about is never to appear to be using high pressure. If you do, you're going to turn customers off immediately. I had a young girl say to me the other day, 'Edna, the one thing I like about you is that after you show the product, and you explain it, you then let me decide. You shut up and don't use any sales pressure. I can't stand high-pressure salespeople.' Now, I've got others who simply can't make a decision to buy without my helping them a little. So with these customers, I have to nudge a little, but I wouldn't call it 'high pressure.' For example, I always make it a point to try to sell some more merchandise when I make a delivery. Some of them will say, 'Edna, don't bother to show me a thing. I know I don't need anything today.' I'll take out the catalogue and say, 'Let's just look through this together. We've got a lot of new items today, and of course you'll want to know about our specials.' But I always make sure that it's a low-keyed, soft sale.''

Edna doesn't get too many phone calls, because she's rarely home between nine in the morning and ten at night. If her customers could have the slightest complaint about her, it would have to be that they can never catch her when she's in. Despite this single deficiency, she tells everyone, ''Don't be afraid to call me. I'm just as far away as your phone. I'm your Avon Lady, and if I don't come when you need me, just call, and I'll be right out.'' While there's no doubt about Edna's sincerity when she tells a customer to call her, most of them have come to realize that Edna is unlikely to be home when she could be working.

''I guess you can call it an obsession with me,'' she confesses. ''But I feel that it's my obligation to my girls that I make my calls whenever it is humanly possible. I can recall one extremely icy day when the driving conditions were simply vicious, and each of my daughters called to advise me to stay home. Even my husband called from school and said, 'Honey, don't you dare go out today. The roads are a sheet of ice.' Well, I didn't listen to them, and on my way up somebody's steep driveway, my legs went out from under me, and my case went flying up in the air. I landed flat on my back, and I knew that I was seriously hurt. But I continued to work straight through the day. Late that afternoon, my husband was driving by and happened to see me getting out of my car. I could hardly breathe, and I told him about my accident. Although I should have listened to him, I didn't stop and even went out that evening after supper. It just so happened that I called on a lady who was a nurse, and when I reached down to pick up something and she saw how much pain I was in, she screamed, 'Edna, what's wrong?' I told her what had happened, and she put some bandages on me. She said that I surely must have broken some ribs and ordered me to see a doctor the next day.

"Well, the next morning I went to see my doctor, and the X rays showed that I had three broken ribs. He gave me the dickens for continuing to work and told me to stay in bed for several days. The next morning, I was determined to work, so I went to my car and had to lift my leg with my hands in order to get into the driver's seat. I went over a bump in the road and tears came to my eyes, it hurt so much. But I didn't stop, and in a few days the soreness went away and I felt fine."

Edna had another experience which would have caused most salespersons to take time off from working without even the strictest boss being able to complain. "A few years ago," Edna recalls, "my husband suffered a heart attack. He was on a very rigid diet, and I had to prepare special meals for him. Well, he was on my mind, and during one of my calls I had to go to my car to get something out of the trunk. Again it was an icy day, and I slipped and fell on my right arm. I went back in and announced, 'I'm sorry, but I'm going to have to go home. I just fell, and I know that I broke my arm.' Of course, the lady felt bad and offered me help, but I explained that I had to get home to fix a special diet dinner for Harold. When I got home, I didn't want to startle him, but when he took one look at my arm, he got dressed and rushed me to the doctor's office.

"We get some pretty rough weather in Minnesota, and the doctor told me that I was his fifth patient that day who had broken some bones on the ice. When he informed me that I had a broken arm, I cried, 'My goodness, how can an Avon Lady work with a broken arm? This is the worst thing that could have happened to me!' Of course, he assured me that there were many worse things that could have happened, but he announced that the cast would remain on my right arm at least eight weeks. His orders were 'No work.' I went home, and I must confess it's one of the few times in my life that I felt really depressed. The following afternoon, I couldn't take the confinement any longer, so I took a pain pill and made my calls. I was only able to carry a small case, and at first I had to have my customers fill out their own orders. They were very patient with me. Within a few days, however, I was able to write with my left hand, and my business got back to normal."

When Edna is asked what motivates her to drive herself to such extremes, she replies, "I offer a service to my girls, and I never want them to think I would let them down. I want them to know that they can depend on me. So often, I hear them complain about other fly-by-night salespersons who never came back again like they promised. If customers are going to deal with an Avon Representative, it's highly important that she come by regularly, because if she doesn't, well, she's not going to give them the service they require.

"I guess the nicest compliment my girls could pay me," Edna adds, "is when they answer the door on one of those miserable, bitter cold nights and they say, 'Edna! I just don't believe it. *Only Edna would come here tonight!* There's not another person in the world who would be out in this weather. Come right on in, Edna.' I guess it's the warm feeling I get when I walk into their homes, and I know how happy they are to see me." She ponders a bit, then softly adds, "That's a wonderful feeling."

An individual has to enjoy what he or she does to put in the long hours Edna devotes to her Avon career. And this devotion also requires a strong belief in the company's product. Edna is the first person to tell you how much she enjoys her work; she even talks about another Avon Lady who's now eighty years old and still selling Avon products. "That's another thing I think is so great about what I do." Edna grins. "This is the kind of work I can do for the rest of my life." Just the thought of retirement makes her cringe. "I love everything about this work," she says. "I love my products, and I love the company. I get so excited when I talk about Avon, my enthusiasm becomes contagious. I live it, I eat it, and it's my life. I know that it shouldn't be, but it is.

"I believe in my products 100 percent," Edna emphatically states. "And my sincerity has to come across to my girls, so then they believe in Avon too. Besides, one of Avon's greatest selling points is that they'll guarantee every product I sell. This is truly a great selling feature, because if any girl doesn't want to keep what I sell her, she'll get a full refund with no arguments. Of course, I don't get but one or two returns a month; however, it's great for my morale to have that guarantee behind me."

In a section of North St. Paul, Minnesota, there are 600 homes where the lady of the house can be absolutely certain of two guarantees. First, Avon will stand behind every product that their Avon Representative sells. Second, although it is not in writing, they can be sure that their Avon Representative, Edna Larsen, will personally guarantee that they will always receive the best service she can give them.

8

Martin D. Shafiroff

(LEHMAN BROTHERS KUHN LOEB)

"Selling convictions via the telephone..."

Martin D. Shafiroff is a partner of Lehman Brothers Kuhn Loeb, Incorporated,* one of the nation's most prestigious investment banking firms. For the twelve month period ending September 30, 1977, his gross commissions were approximately $1.5 million, perhaps the highest of all retail producers in the United States.

Martin joined Lehman Brothers in 1969 and worked in the securities division as a broker, advising both institutional and individual accounts. His main responsibility today is working with individuals throughout the country, advising and recommending investments in securities, real estate, and tax shelters. It is believed that he deals with more board chairmen and presidents of corporations than any other broker in America today. In addition, many of his clients are professional entertainers.

He began his career in investments with Eastman Dillon Union Securities Company (now Blyth Eastman Dillon & Company) in 1966. Prior to entering the securities field, he was a salesman for a small industrial company. In October 1977, Martin became a

---

*The investment banking firms of Lehman Brothers and Kuhn Loeb were merged in December, 1977.

partner of Lehman Brothers. He is currently the only broker-partner in the 125-year-old firm.

He has given numerous lectures on the art of selling, the utilization of time, and the art of investing. Martin has been the subject of feature articles in the *Wall Street Journal* and the prestigious *Institutional Investor* magazine.

Martin was born in Brooklyn, New York, on July 22, 1938. He was graduated in 1962 from City College of the City University of New York, where he majored in finance and investments. He is single and lives in New York City. He is an avid squash and paddleball player.

Martin Shafiroff probably sells more securities each year than any other retail stockbroker in the United States. In the twelve-month-period ending September 30, 1977, he sold nearly $300 million worth of securities, or $1.2 million every working day.

Since he sells to individuals, not to institutions, he is obviously dealing with a highly successful clientele who generate large personal incomes. He probably has more chairmen of the board and presidents of substantial corporations as clients than anybody else in the country. He is based at Lehman Brothers' New York headquarters, but estimates that as many as 80 percent of his clients live out of state. In fact, he estimates that he's met only 25 percent of them in person. This means that Martin sells hundreds of thousands of dollars in securities over the telephone to individuals he's never even shaken hands with. To put it another way, if all 1,200 of his clients were to be assembled in a large hall to pay tribute to this dynamic stockbroker, Martin would know only about 300 of them by sight. The others would appear to be total strangers.

Of course, those 900 clients would be strangers in appearance only. As Martin puts it, "Over a period of time, a very close relationship develops between us. It's an almost philosophical relationship, because we're communicating on a highly important subject—how to properly handle his investments. In this sense, a very strong bond evolves.''

The soft-spoken stockbroker explains, ''I have found that many highly successful executives are very effective in giving you information and defining the future of their corporation, but they are not very efficient investors. This is because they're totally involved in their corporate effort, and consequently they tend to overlook their personal investment affairs, which should be equally important. Sometimes such individuals assign the responsibility to others, and they don't even inspect or evaluate their investments. Quite frankly, *they need my help.*

''So I work with a client who is willing and interested in preserving and building his capital. In my work, I seek out what can be considered a value area, and I determine where a gap has been created in the marketplace. Since I look for values, I continually review securities, foreign currencies, gold, silver, corporate and municipal bonds, and real estate, and I try to find special situations or special timing for investments in these groups. My feeling is that an investment vacuum exists in America today. Institutions are buying into a limited number of companies, and because individual interest in securities has declined, there are magnificent companies with substantial book values which are selling at four and five times earnings and are giving high cash yields to the investor. These companies have outstanding returns on capital and on equity, but they lack publicity and sponsorship. In my opinion, this area offers the greatest investment potential in the years ahead. I believe that many of these companies could not be duplicated today for two or three times their market value, but one must have patience in these investments until recognition comes. When that time does come, the potential on the upside is quite dramatic. Therefore, I have a strategy and philosophical approach to what I am doing. I find an investment which meets these requirements. I am now prepared to present both my approach and my investment suggestion.''

There is a pause as Martin carefully chooses his words. ''I

MARTIN D. SHAFIROFF

believe that you must develop a very strong conviction to a philosophy, and only then can you superimpose that philosophy on
the people you talk to. I am interested in values, wherever those
values may be, and because my clients understand values they
can relate to my philosophy.

"I want to emphasize the importance of having conviction. All
great business successes have strong convictions in what they are
doing. Essentially, the first person whom you must sell to if you
want to succeed is yourself. I believe this is vital. When you
believe in what you are doing, the other party evaluating your
comments is going to react accordingly. For this reason, I believe
that an individual must seek out, that is, study, review, and
analyze the entire investment spectrum until he can come up with
a product and a strategy for which he can develop strong convictions.

"Now, product and conviction are only half of my success
formula; the other half stresses cold calls and contacts. The con-
version of these cold calls to legitimate prospects, that is, prospects who will have an interest in my philosophy, then converting
these prospects into accounts, then building on those accounts, is
my constant goal. The final result is building investment
portfolios for all of my accounts.

"Every day I look at that formula," Martin explains, "and it
gives me direction on where I should be going and what I should
be doing. It's written out in front of me so I can review it. Having
such a game plan is like having an alarm, and I look at it twenty-
five to thirty times a day. I continually ask myself, 'What am I
doing? Why am I doing it? Is it essential?' Over and over, I'll
repeat these questions to myself, and in doing so, I will then
eliminate whatever is nonessential. I believe that corporations, in
attempting to bring written or oral data to the individual, create so
many nonessential items that in the attempt to create good will,
the corporation reduces the effective selling time of the individual. Therefore, I always place my attaché case next to my
desk. Then, whenever nonessential material appears, I put it in
the attaché case, for review during my non-selling hours.

"My selling time is whenever I can contact people. Now that

doesn't necessarily imply only when the market is open. Most of my contact work is done during the day, and this means that a fair amount of my work and reading must be done in the early morning and at night. So, I usually get into the office by eight in the morning and I'm out at about seven in the evening.

"I always remind myself of a study I made on using time in this business. The average person spends relatively little time actually selling. He's reading publications, reviewing every memo that crosses his desk, going out to lunch with his buddies, and doing many other nonproductive activities. In other words, I concluded that he is only utilizing approximately thirty minutes of his selling day asking for the order.

"That's right, his customer contact time is only thirty minutes of his entire working day." Martin shakes his head. "Now, if the average contact time is a half hour, and I can increase it to four or five hours, well, as you can readily see, the leverage involved is quite dramatic. I am essentially my own corporation. I'm the chairman of the board, and I also sweep the floors at the end of the day. Therefore, I must be very sensitive in allotting my time. I have an analytical background, and therefore I analyze every task and continually search for a better way of doing whatever I have to do."

Martin has three assistants. One helps contact clients and prospective clients. Another does investigative work such as gleaning information on prospective clients, and the third assists him in handling the backup work after a transaction occurs. Their work is intermingled, and it's a joint effort. The teamwork is geared to provide Martin with more time to think, and it gives him a greater return on his time.

With the Shafiroff team in full gear, Martin is able to average sixty calls to clients and prospects each day. Eighty percent of his calls will be long distance; some will be to prospective clients, people he's never spoken with before. Even though Martin is the number one man in his field, he still is continually prospecting for new accounts (unlike, for example, the physician who has a "closed practice"). "I don't consider it a good day's work," Martin insists, "unless I have qualified three new accounts. In order to be successful, you must constantly build your business, even though you already have a good one. Every day, in addition to communicating with my existing clients, it is vital that I communicate with new people. Through communicating, I attempt to convert the prospects to clients. That's the life blood of the business.

"You know"—Martin pauses—"so many brokers say they're going to stop attempting to develop new business and concentrate on existing accounts so they won't neglect their present clients. That's bad. They'll lose their momentum, and that's what I consider the key to success. Of course, one reason why I don't have their problem is the way I approach investing. I'm not involved in active trading; I'm essentially looking for long-term investments and having my clients take a substantial position in a company. Because I'm not interested in aggressive trading, my clients become accustomed to building positions over a period of time, and we may make only four or five investments during the course of a year. So, as a value buyer, I'm not really involved in day-to-day communication with my clients. Of course, with their high incomes, they're naturally going to be interested in long-term investments which offer capital gains.

"I constantly tell my client that if he cannot say he would be willing to buy the entire company, then he shouldn't be investing in it. Because I am interested in values, I show him that these companies could not be duplicated for two or three times their market value. And, as an astute businessman, he readily recognizes that fact. We can communicate very clearly because we think along the same wavelength when we talk about values.

"Also, I want to interject what I believe to be very important." He deliberately chooses every word. "My first consideration is the preservation of principal. I think that there's too much emphasis on maximizing returns. But due to the present tax structure, it's far more difficult to build capital than in the past, so we must make every attempt to preserve it. The first strategic question I ask is 'Do I have some measure of the risk?' Once I can measure that risk, I concentrate on the rewards. Now I can estimate my downside. I believe in low multiples with high yields and substantial book values, and these investments should minimize my downside.*

"Once I can estimate the downside, I look for those investments which have the maximum upside potential. As I mentioned earlier, some of these stocks are overlooked because they have lost favor with institutions for one reason or another, and individual investors have reduced their commitments to the marketplace. Therefore, I believe in buying assets. I am buying value, yield, and potential growth. And I look for above-average management. I look at the new low list every day rather than the new high list. I look at companies that are being sold down in price. I try to measure capabilities, and if I believe a company has potential to expand in sales and earnings, and if I can purchase these companies at values which cannot be duplicated, then I make my move."

Martin has a definite game plan. He has astutely done his homework, and he's fully prepared to relate his message to his client or a prospect. "I now have a philosophy—a strategy to present to him," Martin explains. "And it's important to point out that I'm not bound by any particular investment vehicle. I can offer securities, corporate or tax-free bonds, real estate, whatever. It's the concept that I am discussing with the individual. And I strongly believe that the individual I am talking with needs my help. He needs advice. He needs guidance.

"When a prospective client says that he already has a big investment in XYZ Company, I might come back with questions such as 'What are the projected next quarter's earnings? What do you think the company will make for the year? What do you think the proper price of the issue should be?' It's an amazing thing, but I have never received a correct answer in my life! It's surprising that these astute businessmen, who dedicate so much of their

*The *downside* means the maximum loss an investor can estimate, expecting the worst to happen. The *upside* means the most gain that can optimistically be expected from an investment. A *stock multiple* means that investment is selling for x times the earnings per share; i.e., if a company earns one dollar per share during one year and the price of the stock is six dollars, then its multiple is six (six times earnings).

lives as technicians and masters of those corporations they manage, do not approach their private investments in the same manner. These people are very sensitive to the market, and they recognize that there are ways to achieve substantial capital gains in a relatively conservative posture. And when I talk to them about substantial discounts to book value, a heavy cash dividend up front while they wait, and the low multiples which these companies are currently selling for, they can recognize the potential perhaps much more than other people in America can. Because of my background in finance and investments, and because I am associated with Lehman Brothers, a firm which they know is prepared to work with their corporation as well as personally assist them in their private investments, I can communicate very effectively with them.''

Martin's initial telephone call to a prospective client, who is generally a top executive with an income in excess of $250,000, will perhaps be from a referral. '' 'Hello, Bill? This is Martin Shafiroff from Lehman Brothers,' '' he demonstrates. '' 'Your name came to my attention from John Brown, who is doing business with me. He suggested that I contact you and bring to your attention the type of work we have been doing together.'

"I tell him that my interest is in value, wherever that value may be, and in whatever markets the values may be. I also mention that I concentrate on special situations. These are most often companies which are selling at low multiples, have high yields, high book values, and have a possibility of getting substantial capital gains. I also explain to him that I always ask, 'What is my risk in order to achieve my results?' I then explain my philosophy about favoring stocks with low multiples that have potential ahead but are currently selling at five or six times earnings, and I tell him I believe in unloading at perhaps ten or eleven times earnings. I also explain that the weakness in my formula is that it sometimes takes a reasonable period of time before the recognition factor comes. The strength in my formula is concentrating on high yields and low multiples, which limits my downside.''

Martin looks serious, as he says in a low voice, "Again, I talk about conviction, but it comes from the fact that I do my homework so thoroughly. I personally have a difficult time understanding why an issue selling at sixteen times earnings can later sell at twenty-one times earnings. But I have a much better handle on why a company selling at four or five times earnings can sell at seven, eight, or nine times earnings.

"I put a tremendous amount of effort into finding the right companies for my clients to invest in. Using Lehman's research, I review securities like one might review a work of art—a fine painting for instance. Each particular investment has its own features and characteristics. And I firmly believe that no one should make an investment unless he's able to purchase an outstanding asset at an extremely reasonable price. I put a great deal of emphasis on the preserving of principal and getting a combined return on the dollars put out. I remember a conversation I overheard a few years back when two money managers were discussing the handling of a certain account. One stated that he would try to get a 10 percent return, and the other said he would attempt a 14 percent return. Neither of them spoke about the jeopardy which was being placed on the principal in order to achieve those returns."

When Martin is on the telephone, everything he does has a definite purpose. For instance, he jots down the name of his client's secretary. He always calls her by name. "I treat every person as an individual. Besides, there's many little helpful things his secretary can do for you, and she'll more than likely have an influence on her boss. So you want her on your side. After all, it certainly can't hurt, can it?

"Another thing about the secretary, I always state my name and company when I start talking with her, and I do it nicely, so she'll announce me in a favorable way. Sometimes, just her enthusiasm in telling the executive that I am on the wire can make a difference. For example, if she didn't like the person calling, she might say, 'Oh, that Mr. Jones is on the phone, should I tell him you're busy?' But if she's in the caller's corner, she can say it in an approving fashion, such as 'I'm sorry to interrupt, sir, but Mr. Shafiroff is on the telephone, and it sounds important. He would like to speak with you.' "

Although it's normally difficult for a salesman to call a president or the chairman of the board of a major corporation and get through to him, Martin professes that he generally has little trouble. Many times the individual is busy, but he's more than likely to return the call. Martin attributes his exceptional telephone reception to using the name of a friend who has recommended the prospective client, and to Lehman Brothers' prestigious influence with executives of publicly owned companies.

Undoubtedly, there's also a psychological advantage in calling an individual long distance from one of Wall Street's most respected investment banking firms. "I must confess," Martin admits, "that a busy executive is more likely to get on the phone with me than with a local stockbroker he has never met. You know, the 'expert from New York' image, I suppose."

Martin believes his presentation is not only different from the typical securities salesman's, but much more effective. "Almost every presentation is divided into three parts. There's the introduction, the middle, and the end. I find that most people concentrate on the middle. If, for example, a typical presentation takes twenty minutes to deliver, the average salesman will spend the majority of his time, perhaps as much as fifteen minutes, presenting the reasons why the prospect should make the investment. If he spends approximately three minutes making his introduction, he'll only spend two minutes making a request for the order.

"I like to turn the proportions around." Martin smiles. "As much as 60, maybe 70, percent of the time should be in the request for the order. I start with a request that a transaction be made with a particular company, and if the individual is contemplating making that investment, I immediately flash images of why the investment is an outstanding one. Rather than spend all of my time in presenting reasons alone, I interweave these reasons with the request for the order.

"Let's take XYZ Corporation, for example, a large manufacturing company. Instead of spending much time on the presentation, I list five reasons why the investment should be made, and then I request the order. If the individual hesitates, I say, 'John, do you know of any other company selling at four and a half times this year's earnings which has a 16.7 percent return on equity? The company has a couple hundred million dollars in working capital, and its book value is substantially higher than the market value. Could we duplicate this company at two or three times its present market price? The answer is *no!*'

"In other words," Martin emphasizes, "*get to the point.* I'm asking the individual to make a substantial investment because I believe in the product. And I believe that he will ultimately make money in it. Therefore, as quickly as possible, I give him the reasons why he should make the investment. I then say, 'John, I believe you should own 5,000 shares of XYZ.' He may reply, 'It sounds like a good idea; let me think about it.' I then ask him if there's anything I overlooked. The key ingredient which I believe now separates me from the run-of-the-mill securities salesman is that I believe that I must penetrate any defense mechanisms. I believe that an order must be asked for more than once. I must find out the real reason behind the individual's hesitation. For example, if he's agreed with me that he too considers values a good motive for making an investment, then I must penetrate his defenses and make him want to invest by demonstrating that I have value for him.

"I continue to probe. I ask, 'Is there anything that I may have overlooked in my presentation?' He may answer, 'What I really would like to do is review my funds.' Now I have a specific reason. I tell him that I called him because I believe the price is advantageous and he should make an investment at this particular time. I may then suggest it's important that at least a portion of his funds be used to take advantage of the present price. I am now trying to create a mental compromise. Perhaps the individual has a minimum amount in mind. I suggest that we take advantage at least of that amount.

"As you can see," he recapitulates, "the major error of most salespeople is they divide their sales talk into three distinct parts. The beginning, the middle (the presentation), and the close. I differ because I reduce the beginning by making it a relatively contained presentation. I spend about three minutes on my introduction, and then only three or four minutes on the reasons why, and then I devote the remaining time, which could run twelve to fifteen minutes, on the request for the order. This difference has a dramatic effect on the business that I am able to develop. I do want to repeat, however, that while the individual is considering my request for the order, I constantly flash the images for the reasons why he should take affirmative action. So, I do not break my presentation into the typical three parts. I have an introduction, and I list five reasons why the investment should be made. Now I recognize the request for the order as *the moment of truth,* and I simultaneously state my reasons why the order should be executed.''

Martin also believes that the average broker only asks for the order a single time, but he will ask three times. ''I believe that often the individual is not thinking about the concept, just the product. He sets up his defense mechanism because he doesn't want to part with his dollars, and often the securities salesman will accept an unreal reason why the executive turned down a request to execute the transaction.

''I think this kind of reaction is due to a semi-hypnotic defense mechanism which is built into many potential investors. I'm not implying any deep psychological motives. I simply believe that because the average executive is asked for his money so many times, he develops a defense mechanism which automatically rejects, rather than accepts, requests on how he should invest his money. I mean, let's face it, over a period of years, this potential investor has been inundated by possibilities. It's happening to him every day. Perhaps his insurance agent just discussed the possibilities of increasing his life insurance program. His wife wants to buy a second home. He may be considering buying another car. Maybe a competing broker is recommending a bond purchase. It's impossible for the potential investor to give in to all of these demands, because he has a limited amount of capital. So he's developed his defense mechanism, and sometimes he himself may not even be aware of it. But you have to realize that the executive will say no to investment requests many more times than he will, or for that matter, can afford to, say yes. With this thought in mind, I firmly believe that the best way to penetrate his defense mechanism is by taking a philosophical and strategic approach. Taking it one step further, instead of thinking in terms of selling securities, bonds, or real estate, I believe I'm in the business of selling philosophies and concepts.

"As I said earlier, I'm dealing with executives who have very strong feelings for concepts. They are people who, through hard work and ability, have become the best in whatever they do. Therefore, they're looking for something that's different, something that's unique and something that makes sense to them. These individuals can understand a philosophical and strategic approach far more quickly than the average investor can."

Martin pauses briefly, then adds, "I find that when most people receive an objection on the telephone, they hang up. Sure, they ask for the order, but when the individual says, 'I'm not interested,' or 'I want to think it over,' that's the end of the conversation. I think the successful person in this business has to be able to penetrate any objection and find out why the prospect objects. As I indicated, this defense mechanism has layers which have to be removed. My formula is that in order to be successful, you have to be on the road to success and stay there. Now when you make a presentation and ask for the order, the individual might put you off; he might say, for instance, "Let me think about it.' Well, that takes you off the road. You're sidetracked! It's a generalized statement, and in order to overcome it, you must convert it into a specific objection. This is necessary or you won't be able to understand his reasons for not taking affirmative action. If the individual wants to think about it, I'll ask, 'Are you thinking about it because I might have overlooked some salient point in my presentation? Is there something else you want to know?' He might answer, 'No, I have to check my cash position.' It is very important for me to put that conversation back on the road again. And once I do, I will ask for the order a second time.

"If he's uncertain of his cash position, I'll ask him if he has a minimum or a maximum investment in mind. I'll suggest that it would be advantageous to make the minimum investment now. But, as I have repeatedly stated, I must believe in the thing I'm doing. I have to believe that the current market value is an advantageous price for the individual, and I must believe that Lehman Brothers' recommendation will ultimately be reflected in the price of the stock.

"It's my feeling that the individual perceives a concept, and if he really believes what I am saying, he's capable of making an investment at that time. So it's simply a matter of developing my convictions, and then expressing them to him. Now, if an individual says, 'I want to think about it,' I think the next questions, as I mentioned before, are 'What does he want to think about?' Does he want to think about it because he doesn't have enough facts? And if I think so, I ask him that. If he wants additional information, I'll give it to him, but he must be brought back on the track. I will ask for the order a second and a third time if I think it's necessary. Sure, it's easy to execute orders when the individual goes along with everything I say. It's when he gives an objection that the average salesman is taken off the road. I know that I must then attempt to surround the objection and put him back on the road. I have made studies which show that the person who makes three requests for the order instead of one request will be eminently more successful."

Martin continues in a low voice. "I also firmly believe that listening is a vital part of selling. And I try to involve the other party in the conversation as much as I can. I may, for example, pull him into the conversation by asking, 'Would you agree that a company with these returns, this growth rate, and with a multiple of four and a half times earnings is an unusual investment?' I also believe that it's very important to get him to reply in the affirmative. When he answers yes, I will wait to see if there's anything else he wants to add. You know, it's very difficult for an individual to say yes four or five times, and then say no when you request the order. If he says no at the end of my presentation, I may very well say, 'Look, you have agreed that this is an exceptional investment. You've agreed to all of my comments on why the order should be executed. Now I think it's important to follow through on this and for you to be an investor in this particular company.''

On the surface, it seems amazing that anyone could convince another individual over the telephone to invest his personal funds in amounts running as high as six and seven figures. This is particularly astounding since it may be the first time that Martin has ever talked to him on the telephone (as noted previously, he has never met many of his clients in person). Martin doesn't think it's so astounding. As he puts it, ''Because my concentration is so heavy on conviction, and I believe that my method is successful, I convey my thoughts to the individual on the other end of the line. I know that the executive is going to want to do business with me if he feels strongly that I can make money for him in a relatively conservative manner. I don't think that there's any person I deal with, or for that matter that I speak to, who wouldn't be willing to invest with me if he had favorable experiences with the work I have done. I often tell the executive that I am sure he would agree with me that nobody has a monopoly on ideas. I explain to him that my work is a specialty, and I will not be calling him with the same investment his local broker calls him about. I have something to offer him that's unique. If he has a strong loyalty to his local broker, which many people have, I comment that if I'm successful for him, he will have more money to invest with me, and with his local broker as well.''

Martin places a great deal of emphasis on his conviction factor, and he believes in really researching the products that he recommends so he is certain that he can offer values to his clients. ''I feel that a person can't be a jack of all trades,'' he explains. ''In today's business world, you have to be specialized. I think one of the problems many men in my field have is that they cater to the whims of the potential investor. If the individual does not perceive my concept, or for one reason or another he's unwilling to accept it, I suggest that he's probably better doing business with someone else. I think that I have to do that, because if I don't I'll lose my conviction, and that will force me to cater to many needs and then not be outstanding at anything. I would rather be outstanding in one way of doing things than be mediocre at ten ways of doing things."

Martin takes a strong posture in his dealings with his clients, who are some of the most dynamic executives in the country. Evidently it pays off. It's not easy to handle supercharged executives with enormous egos, but he has learned to work effectively with this type of individual. "I consider their egos to be a positive factor," he claims. "I take that ego and I blend in my philosophy. I say, "Look, you are the manager of a corporation. You, above everyone else, surely recognize value. If you were given the opportunity to make this investment, and if you had all the cash proceeds, I would predict that you would probably be willing to buy the entire company.' Again, I'm talking their language, because businessmen recognize value!

"Well, I believe that the man on the other end of the phone hears what I am telling him. And he recognizes that I know my product quite well, and he appreciates it. Once he develops confidence in me, he's going to want me advise him on his investments."

Martin became a securities salesman in 1966 with Eastman Dillon, after a three-year period as an industrial salesman, during which he averaged $8,000 a year. He joined Lehman Brothers in 1969, and by 1971, his fifth year in the securities business, his annual income was $325,000. Much of his success is due to his tenacity in driving himself in an industry which is among the most highly competitive businesses in the world. "I find that too many people are concerned with failure," he says. "Their preoccupation with failure reflects their attitudes, and its image is far greater than the word itself. I believe that rejection is part of the key to success. If the individual can gain perspective and can understand that over a period of time he will continually upgrade the quality of his work, then he will begin to find the so-called key to success. Therefore, in my opinion, if one is able to use failure in a constructive manner, he will be structuring the building blocks to success.

"I work on a mathematical formula. I know that for each person who rejects my concepts due to his past experiences and his built-up defense mechanism, there is another individual who is willing to accept my concepts in order to build his financial success. I believe in this very strongly. Success is a learning process which relates to the building blocks. In the securities industry, I think that an individual must set up a target for the number of telephone calls he is going to make, and then it's reduced to a mathematical formula. Over a period of time, by carefully analyzing his rejections, he will refine his techniques to a degree where they will eventually succeed. And this is precisely what I did."

Martin leans forward. "Another good way to learn from what you are doing is to be sure to include the word 'why' in your vocabulary. When a person says no, I believe that it is usually a defense mechanism. I will respond by asking, 'Why?' I know I'm going to get a response. And I listen very carefully to his answer. Often when he states that he doesn't have the funds, I interpret it to mean I haven't been persuasive enough. I just haven't been able to communicate with him.

"I'll also analyze my presentation when I haven't convinced a prospective client to share my concepts with me. Then I try to make a determination of what improvements should be made in it. I will usually develop a better understanding of what went wrong. And I know that mathematically I will translate one out of every three calls into a transaction, so every no gets me that much closer to a yes.

Another good quality about Martin is his perseverance. He is the first to admit, "I am very persistent, but I firmly believe that it pays off. I recall one individual whom I called perhaps fifteen times before I finally got through to him. In fact, he even commented that I was one of the most persistent people that he had ever known. And, as it turned out, we were able to do substantial business together.''

By carefully analyzing exactly what he does, Martin has figured out the chances of getting the highest mathematical return for the amount of energy he exerts. He knows, for example, that if a client procrastinates on the phone and wants to think it over, unless he can penetrate the objection, the odds for getting the order are greatly diminished. Martin knows how to maximize his time. He thoroughly understands his product and his client. In summary, Martin is programmed to succeed, and he is quite willing to work long-hours enthusiastically in order to achieve record-breaking results.

Martin is now setting his sights on generating annual commissions in excess of $3 million. Within a year or two, he probably will.

9

J. Michael Curto

(US STEEL)

"The soft selling of hard steel..."

J. Michael Curto is the group vice president–steel of the United States Steel Corporation. His responsibilities include coordinating and directing the activities of the company's four steel-producing divisions and all commercially oriented staff functions.

Mike joined US Steel's sales training program in 1937. He began his career in the Philadelphia sales office, and became a salesman in 1939, serving in that capacity until 1943, when he entered the United States Navy. He was discharged as a lieutenant (j.g.) and returned to US Steel in 1946.

He was appointed assistant to the manager of sales in the Pittsburgh sales office in 1950, and became assistant manager two years later. In 1957, he was assigned to the New York district sales office as manager. On January 1, 1964, Mike was appointed vice president–sales, eastern area, and he assumed the position of vice president–marketing on March 1, 1972.

On January 1, 1974, four steel divisions were established within US Steel, with responsibility for coordination of production and sales of steel products in each geographical area. Mike was appointed vice president and general manager of the eastern steel division at that time.

He was named to the newly created position of group vice president–steel, his current position, on April 1, 1975.

Mike is a member of the American Iron and Steel Institute and serves on the board of trustees of Shadyside Hospital, the board of directors of the Greater Pittsburgh Chamber of Commerce, the board of governors of the Harvard Business School Association of Pittsburgh, and the executive committee of the Princeton Alumni Association of Western Pennsylvania. He's also active with the Pittsburgh Symphony and headed its 1977 industrial campaign drive committee.

He was born in Latrobe, Pennsylvania, on August 3, 1914. He graduated from Kiski Preparatory School, and in 1936 graduated from Princeton University, where he majored in political science and pre-law. He's also a graduate of the Advanced Management Program at the Harvard Business School.

Mike and his wife, Marylou, live in Pittsburgh. They have a son, Thomas, and a daughter, Christine Tullo. Mike is an avid golfer, and he and his wife spend much of their leisure time at their second home near Palm Beach, Florida.

United States Steel Corporation is the largest steel company in the United States and one of the largest in the world. There are four lines of business groups at US Steel. It is Mike Curto's responsibility to head the largest and most prestigious one—steel, which accounts for approximately 75 percent of the corporation's $9 billion in annual sales and revenue. Mike's seemingly awesome job makes him accountable to the company's president for the profitability of its most important product; and as the group vice president, he coordinates all activities involving the manufacturing, distributing, and marketing of steel.

Currently, US Steel has a sales force of 190 salesmen who sell about $7 billion worth of steel each year. That's $35 million per man—perhaps the highest dollar volume per man of any sales organization its size in the world. A further breakdown of this giant corporation reveals that it has an estimated 10,000 customers, and 20 percent of them buy 80 percent of the tonnage sold. And, of course, there's only one General Motors, the largest buyer of steel in the world! Due to unique qualities of the product and the large dollar amounts of it sold per customer, there's a fascinating story behind US Steel's selling techniques and philosophies that Mike Curto has been instrumental in implementing during the past forty years.

J. MICHAEL CURTO

Shortly after graduating from Princeton University in 1936, Mike became a salesman for US Steel. Actually he began his selling career while attending Princeton on a scholastic scholarship ("I was probably the only guy in the thirties out of western Pennsylvania who wasn't on a football scholarship"); he was a sales agent for four New York newspapers and several magazines on the campus. "I was the agent for the New York *Herald Tribune*, the New York *World-Telegram*, the New York *Sun*, and the *New York Times*. I also had magazines such as *Time* and *Fortune*. I set up a delivery system so the students could get the morning and evening papers delivered to their doors. It was a great experience, and that's how I broke into sales.

"You know," he adds, "I made $2,000 during my senior year, and when I started my first job upon my graduation, I was paid seventy-two dollars a month! I went to work for a man who was starting a new sports magazine, and because of the distribution experience I picked up in college, he hired me. It was a small organization, so I did everything. I was in charge of advertising sales, as well as distribution, and I even did some reporting. The operation didn't make it, because it was a monthly magazine, and nothing is as old as sports news that is thirty days old! Incidentally, we called the magazine *Sports Illustrated;* the title was later sold to Time, Inc., and it succeeded as a weekly.

"During the spring of 1937, I was pinch-hitting as a reporter covering the P.G.A. golf tournament in Pittsburgh, and an old friend who had been instrumental in getting me my scholarship at Princeton told me how upset he was that I had received such a fine education and was involved in sports reporting. He suggested that I interview with US Steel while I was in Pittsburgh. There were 500 applicants at Carnegie Steel in Pittsburgh applying for the job, and another 500 from Illinois Steel in Chicago; you see, that was prior to the merging and formation of US Steel as it is presently structured. They narrowed the field to seven men for six positions, and I received a telegram in New York requesting that I be in Pittsburgh in two days for the final decision. Well, we all appeared in the office of the vice president of sales, and everyone knew that one guy wasn't going to make it. I survived that one! And, as it turned out, the one who didn't make it was hired for the next training program the following year." Mike did make it—and he's been making it big with US Steel ever since.

All but one of those seven young men hired as salesmen made lifetime careers with US Steel. This kind of longevity is significant in illustrating the selling philosophy of the company. Unlike most sales organizations, there is very little turnover of salesmen at US Steel; the reason for this is the company's approach in developing a salesman. "We have a very thorough training program," Mike explains. "A great deal of a new man's time will be spent developing manufacturing knowledge. He will spend most of his time learning manufacturing techniques in the mill. This will be as an observer, because it would be impractical for him to actually work on-the-job for short assignments of a month or so, although I have toyed with the idea.

"We'll move the trainee through the company's different mills, which produce various products," Mike continues. "And, of course, we'll give him sales training, consisting of some on-the-job training, that is, actually going out in the field with an experienced salesman."

The distinguished-looking steel executive sits back, and in a soft voice explains, "We've made a major change in our organizational pattern since I started with the company. You see, sales used to be a separate part of the organization, so we had a distinctly different set of people in the operations end of the business. The company was then structured so a field salesman worked his way straight up the ladder to executive vice president of sales. His only function was selling, and he had no exposure to the operations end of the business. Likewise, the other side of the organization broke a new trainee into the business as a mill production man, and he worked his way through operations, on a straight line to executive vice president of operations.

"Well, we've changed our organization so that we have a division vice president and general manager who is responsible for both operating and sales, and we have smaller groups which consist of both operating and selling people working together. Now, working as a closely knit unit, these groups report to the vice president–general manager of that division. I've been quite instrumental in developing this cross-pollination program. I like to refer to it as a rounding-out program, whereby we develop a man so he has full exposure to the entire scope of our business. Regardless of whether he starts out in sales or operations, we begin to round him out by exposing him to different facets of the company. For example, someone who starts out in sales will spend some portion of his career in the manufacturing end of the business, and we'll swing him into finance as we take him through the organization. We'll give him a broad base, so he will be capable of working with different people within the company, say, for example, with an individual who has an engineering background.

"We're trying to get our people oriented to the total business venture, so that when they make decisions, their broad knowledge of the entire profit picture will help them make the proper decisions," Mike emphasizes. "When you get a nine-billion-dollar corporation the size of US Steel, it's very important to have decision-making people throughout the chain of command."

This rounding-out program offers the person who has had a good track record in either operations or sales many opportunities for middle management positions, and provides for further advancement as he or she pursues a career with US Steel. These vast opportunities for well-trained personnel have had much to do with the low turnover rate for individuals beginning their careers in sales.

"Although we don't have commissioned salesmen," Mike says, "our people are highly motivated because we have a promotion system which is based on an individual's effectiveness. Commissioned salesmen, while they can earn a high amount during one year, start all over again the following year. With giant customers like General Motors, where so many of our people are involved—including our board chairman—there's no way we can pay commissions to one salesman. We do, however, have bonuses which I believe provide good incentive. Of course, with the many opportunities for advancement that US Steel offers, we believe that our salesmen have ample reason to be highly motivated, even though they don't get commissions.

"We have a unique situation with US Steel," Mike expounds, "because the steel industry has historically had two vertical lines of progression: an individual was either in sales or in operations. And what happened was we developed a very sharp line of demarcation, so the sales guys blamed the boys at the mill for all the problems which occurred with customers, and vice versa. The mill people said, 'You guys in sales don't understand the problem.' So now we've instituted a program which enables everyone to learn and understand the other man's problems, and we're able to get full cooperation from everyone at every level."

It's important to realize that selling steel is quite different from selling other types of products. As Mike puts it, "When you're selling a basic product like steel, as compared to something else, you've got to realize that what we're selling isn't a whole lot different from what our competitor can produce. In steel, we take some iron ore, refine it, and eventually end up with a product of a semi-finished nature. Now, we might have a sheet of steel which will ultimately be formed into a fender for an automobile. Or we might be talking about a structural beam which eventually goes into a building, but you must realize that in neither case are we selling a product to the ultimate consumer.

"Also, remember that we start out with the same pound of iron ore that our competitor does, and while we work hard to have better quality steel, we essentially end up with the same product. Obviously, we improve on it quality-wise, but in the seventy-six years that US Steel has been in business, the improvement has basically been concerned with how a semi-finished product can be made into a more refined end product. And, you have to remember that our competition generally moves along at the same level. So, we don't have the jazz which can be offered in other selling endeavors.

"For example, we don't have the new models every year. We

can't come out with this year's product and spend millions of dollars advertising what we can offer our customer. We don't have the hottest product on the market one year and develop something better for the next. So, while it may appear on the surface that there's not a great deal to sell because the differences in our product and our competitors' seem so insignificant, we have to sell *service*. Our salesman must convince the customer that we're the best in our industry, and that over the long run he's better off doing business with us. A salesman has to develop a customer's confidence; he must believe that US Steel products are not only equal to what the competition sells, but are the best that can be produced in that particular line. And he better be damn sure that the products are as good as he says they are, because he's going to be calling back on that customer many times throughout the year. It's not like selling a product on a one-shot basis. It's different from the salesman who's selling over the counter or on a door-to-door basis. You know, he bangs on a door and only has five minutes to talk with the lady of the house, so he had better make it in a hurry! In our business, the salesman may call on a customer week after week over a period of years, and when a salesman is visiting a customer on such a frequent basis, he can't rely on being a Fancy Dan with a couple of jokes.

"Our salesman must establish a rapport with the buyer," Mike explains. "And, he can't depend on taking him out to lunch, having a couple of drinks with him, or playing a round of golf. Today's purchasing profession consists of top-caliber individuals, and those old days of giving them lunches and entertainment went out with Diamond Jim Brady. And I think that the purchasing man resents that kind of selling. Today's steel salesman has to make the customer feel confident that he is an individual who understands the problems of the business, and I don't care who he's calling on. Whether it's the automotive, appliance, or structural fabricating industry, the salesman has to understand the customer's problems and properly relay them to US Steel management."

There's a pause as Mike ponders. "Several years ago, when I was a sales vice president in the East, I used to call on a major steel buyer who was giving all of their business to another steel company. They were very loyal to our competitor because, when their own company was just beginning, it received financial help from them. I continually called on this company, but I could sense that the owner's loyalty to our competitor was so strong that I would have overstepped my bounds had I tried to aggressively pull him away from them. I could also sense that if I stayed in there, I would eventually get some business.

"I continued to call on him, and we became good personal friends, but still I wasn't getting any business. In a low-key manner, I would subtly sell him on US Steel. Now what did happen was the competing steel company was taken over by a conglomerate, and the new management fired all the customer's old friends. When that happened, he no longer felt any obligation to that company. Well, there I was . . . just sitting there in the wings, very eager to do business with him. And, sure enough, he swung all of the business over to us. I want to point out that all of this took place over a period of two years, and knowing that any kind of selling pressure on my end would have ruined the relationship I was building, well, I played it very low key. I just waited, and when he finally did call to give us the business, we became his major supplier."

Mike sits back, relaxed, and continues. "As I mentioned earlier, our salesman is well trained in the fundamentals of our business, and we expect him to understand the requirements of his customers. Once he's made the contact with the customer, it's very important for him to determine when to bring in our technical people. For example, we have metallurgists who have devoted a lifetime to that end of the steel business. So, if a salesman is selling a flat sheet to General Motors, which plans to put it in a die to form a fender, it's the metallurgist's job to solve any problems. For instance, they might be getting breakage in that fender. The salesman brings in the metallurgist to find out why the steel is breaking in the die, so that the corrections can be made. As you can see, it's a team effort when the salesman gets the right technical people involved in solving the customer's problems.

"Another thing, US Steel has more than a thousand people in its research group, many of whom have doctorates. So the basic product, steel, is just the beginning. What our technical people do for our customer really makes the difference. We take our technical people right to the customer's plant, so they get to know the manufacturing people, and they all become very closely associated. It's really a team effort. And we like for our customers to think of us as being on the same team. We're working with them to solve problems the customer is having in manufacturing. . . . It's important for him to know that we're always right there on the job.

"Now you have to remember," Mike adds, "we have some very qualified competition. And they also have their experts who specialize in metallurgy. But we do believe that we offer the best service in the industry."

There's an air of confidence as Mike speaks. His appearance, conservative dress, and soft manner are more reminiscent of a bank president or a Wall Street stockbroker than the stereotype of a hard-hitting, powerful steel company officer. "As I said earlier, I am the group vice president of steel, and I have both operations and sales under me. You have to understand that we can't run a mill without orders, so I spend a lot of my time and effort in my old bailiwick, sales. And we've just successfully completed a major battle: our campaign against the aluminum beer and soft-drink can. As you may recall, beer and soft-drink cans were originally made of steel, but aluminum with its 'easy-open' lid moved into this business and developed a two-piece aluminum can which could be produced at the rate of 800 per minute. Although aluminum is a more expensive metal than steel, this time factor put them in a more competitive position, as we were only capable of producing 500 to 600 per minute. That may not sound like a major factor, buy when you speak in terms of productivity, the difference is very apparent. And even though steel is a less expensive metal, it was more economical to use aluminum.''

Mike beams. ''I am proud to announce that we were very successful in our campaign, and you'll begin to see that the newest can lines will be making steel rather than aluminum cans. Now, this was a major sales effort, and it took place over a two-year period. We established a research and development team, and we installed special equipment at our research lab to tackle the problem. Steel cans can now be produced at the rate of 900 cans per minute. Then, we went directly to the major brewers and soft-drink people in the country to convince them of the value of the steel can versus the aluminum can. We also had to get the support of the can industry, companies like American Can, Crown Cork and Seal, and National Can. But, of course, it's the brewers and soft-drink companies who buy the cans. It was a long-drawn-out campaign calling on the people at Anheuser Busch, Pabst, Schlitz, and all the big brewers. We had to sell them on the concept that steel would be better than aluminum. So, you see, we developed a product which was comparable to aluminum, but of course steel is a cheaper metal. We figure that our market potential is the fourteen billion aluminum beer cans. This is about 700,000 tons of steel—about $350,000,000 of volume. It is a significant part of our total sales.

''But you have to appreciate the team effort which went into this campaign,'' Mike emphasizes. ''There was a great deal of research so we could develop a pilot can-making line. We had to pool all of our expertise, both in marketing and manufacturing. This involved a lot of research, time, and energy, prior to going out and selling. We had to have something to show them. I think that this is a good example of what I said earlier about why it's necessary to develop our salespeople so they understand the operations end of the steel business and vice versa. This campaign took a great deal of coordination, and only with everyone working together were we able to succeed.''

After a brief pause, Mike goes on. ''There are many special

products which require us to work with a customer in solving a problem. A good example is our teamwork with the automobile industry. We had to put in a separate facility to make the kind of steel which is used for the catalytic converter. And that's a calculated risk, because we never know how long there's going to be a need for the catalytic converter. There's always the possibility that some other technique will be developed to handle automobile exhaust fumes. Another good example of the kind of cooperation we extend to our customers is the galvanized coating the automotive companies have been pressured into offering on their new models. The public demanded that they start making automobiles that won't rust and corrode like the ones which have been manufactured in Detroit. We worked very closely with them, and developed a product in Gary, but let me tell you, it cost us a great deal of money for research and setting up our facility. We had to develop a sheet product which had a super finish that will take all those fancy lacquers, a nice paint job, and then on the inside, where it wouldn't show, was corrosion-resistant. Well, such a product takes a very special application, and it can't be used for any other industry. In this particular case, the automotive people came to us, their supplier, and asked us to solve their problem. Now, instances like this involve a strong coordination effort on the part of our top management.''

US Steel has accepted the premise that the ''little guy'' in American business does not have the corporate resources to continually make his voice heard, so large companies become the major spokesmen for industry in a free-enterprise system. Naturally, US Steel doesn't stand alone in this leadership role, because it is in the best interest of the American economy for major companies from all industries to share the responsibility. It's not unusual for top executives from the company to meet with officials in Washington to discuss issues involving tax reforms or foreign-trade policy, for example, and thereby influence the government decisions. In a broad sense, these activities could be considered ''selling,'' but on a much larger scale, US Steel's involvement goes much further than solely benefiting itself and the steel industry in this country. Every business in America has a stake in the outcome.

At present, there's much concern about Japanese steel being shipped to the United States along with other imports. A worried look appears on Mike's face as he stresses, "This represents a great potential danger not only to the steel industry, but to other industries as well. If our government continues to permit this subsidized competition, our entire free-enterprise system is in jeopardy. And I want to make sure it's understood that it *is* subsidized competition. The Japanese government is clearly subsidizing their steel companies. Consequently, they're able to beat our prices, because they're selling excess steel, which they can't consume in Japan, at prices which are lower than their costs!

"Well, there's a big temptation for our customers to buy their steel at lower prices, especially for our smaller customers whose competition is buying at lower prices," Mike continues. "It's our selling job to convince our customers that in the long run they'll be making a big mistake, because if the American steel companies can't generate the necessary capital for expansion, then eventually all American industries will suffer. First, there will be high unemployment, which affects everyone. If steelworkers are unemployed, they're not going to buy automobiles, appliances, or housing, and that hurts everyone's business. Of course, the bigger issue is that this country must be capable of producing its own steel; we can't become dependent upon other nations to supply us with this basic product. Hell, we can't put ourselves in a position where suddenly there's a shortage of steel because these foreign countries don't want to sell it to America, or, if they do sell it, we'll have to pay exorbitant prices—like we do for oil—because we're dependent upon imports to meet our needs.

"Consequently, we have to sell our customers on the premise that they're going to be in business for a long time, and it's in their best interest to buy American steel, because if we're not around to sell it to them in the future, they might not be able to get it at a reasonable price. So, we get back to that long-term relationship which we develop with our customer. Not only do we offer him our researching, designing, and marketing resources, but also our capacity and availability as a supplier for his company during peak periods when his demand for steel is greatest. So, we're selling him quality, service, and delivery. And he's buying the security of knowing that his company will have a source to supply its needs down the road, because if he's dependent upon steel as a base material for his product, he better make sure that he always can get it!

"To sum it all up," Mike concludes, "I think that the key word is 'confidence.' I believe that we're selling confidence, which the customer must have in the salesman and the company. He's going to feel comfortable doing business with US Steel, because we produce a quality product, and because we are going to be there to supply him during the good times as well as the bad times. He knows that we have the marketing know-how, the research to keep abreast of his requirements and needs, but most important, he can depend on us."

10

William J. Bresnan

(TELEPROMPTER)

"Finding a need and responding to it . . ."

William J. Bresnan is president of the cable television division of
Teleprompter Corporation, the largest cable television company
in the United States. Since 1974, Bill has been senior vice president of Teleprompter Corporation, the parent company. From
July 1972 to May of 1974, he served as interim president of Teleprompter Corporation. In addition, he is a member of the board of
directors and the executive committee of Teleprompter Corporation.

Bill entered the cable television industry in 1958, when he designed and built the system in Rochester, Minnesota. He sub-
sequently supervised the engineering activities of a group of
cable television properties operated by the owners of the
Rochester system. Prior to entering the cable television field, he
was a salesman for a radio and electronics company.

In 1965, Bill was named vice president–engineering, and the
following year he became the executive vice president of the
cable television holdings of Jack Kent Cooke. When the Cooke
systems merged with H & B American Corporation to form the
nation's largest cable TV company in 1968, Bill became executive vice president of H & B American Corporation. H & B merged

into Teleprompter Corporation in 1970, and he was named western vice president of Teleprompter's cable television division. In 1972, he became vice president, assistant to the chairman.

In 1972–73, he was the chairman of the National Cable Television Association. He also chaired its public relations committee for two years and has been a member of the association's executive committee in 1971, 1972, 1973, 1975, 1976, and 1977. Bill was named Man of the Year by *Cable News* for his outstanding service to the cable industry during 1975. Bill is a member of the Institute of Electrical and Electronics Engineers, the Audio Engineering Society, the Society of Motion Picture and Television Engineers, the American Association for the Advancement of Science, the Hollywood Radio and Television Society, and the Society of Cable Television Engineers. He is a member of the Young President's Organization, Inc.

Bill was born in Mankato, Minnesota, on December 5, 1933. He attended Mankato Technical School, Mankato Commercial College, and Winona State College.

Bill and his wife, Barbara, and their six children—Michael, Robert, Daniel, Colleen, Mary, and Maureen—live in Scarsdale, New York. Bill's hobbies are radio history and collecting antique radios.

"We're in a service business," explains Bill Bresnan. "We don't have a long-term contract with our customer. We provide month-to-month service, and he can disconnect it during the month and receive a pro-rata refund. In effect, we're selling on a day-to-day basis, and we have to make sure that our customer feels that he's receiving value so that he'll want to continue doing business with us."

The cable television business isn't as automatic as many people think it is. The customer doesn't simply sign up for the service and send in a monthly check for the rest of his life, as with a utility. If he doesn't feel that he's getting his money's worth, he'll discontinue it. And, although it's a highly technical and regulated industry, cable TV is still very much like any other American business—*effective selling is mandatory!*

Bill has a total commitment to the cable television industry. And undoubtedly his tremendous enthusiasm and love of labor have placed him at the top of one of America's most exciting and fastest-growing industries. As the past chairman of the National Cable Television Association and the industry's Man of the Year, he states with a true pioneering spirit, "This is an exciting time . . . it's a time when we are building a whole industry. It's

WILLIAM J. BRESNAN

most important that we sell our industry to the public as well as to the lawmakers. Cable television is really just being formulated, so we're laying the groundwork for the future. And, of course, we're in an ever-changing business.''

Bill's interest in electronics as a boy in southern Minnesota was the real beginning of his exciting career. "When I was twelve years old, I started fixing the neighbors' radios for extra spending money," he recalls. "Later, I worked in a radio and television shop during my high school days." Bill then spent two years at Mankato Technical School, and soon started his first full-time job as a salesman for an electronics company, selling radio and television supplies. His first real exposure to cable television came in 1955 when his hometown, Mankato, decided to build a system.

"I was selling supplies to radio and television stations"—Bill grins—"and I got wind that there was going to be a cable television system in town, so I immediately contacted the entrepreneurs who were building it. It was an amazing thing, because in those days nobody knew anything about cable TV, and I wanted to be the one to sell them their coaxial cable. I got these big dollar signs in my eyes when I began to think about all those miles of cable installing the system was going to require. The local owner said, 'Fine, we'll be happy to do business with you, but we're only interested in this very special brand of cable. If you can figure out a way to sell it to us, great, we'll buy it from you!'

"Well, I found the manufacturer's rep in the field somewhere out in South Dakota, and I explained to him that I had an opportunity to sell about 120 miles of cable. With that, he made me an instant distributor! Of course, I was selling for a company called Northwest Radio and Electronics, so they actually got the distributorship.

"In order to keep the sales going," Bill recalls, "I had to spend a couple of days each week helping the engineer who was designing and laying out the system. As soon as we finished an area of town, I would write up the bill of materials and process the order. In order to keep my commissions coming in, I gave him as much assistance as possible. We were about halfway through with the project when he had some wife problems and blew town, so I was left with the responsibility of completing the job!

"Well, there I was in this small town in southern Minnesota, and by working on that system, I suddenly became the Minnesota expert." Bill chuckles. "I really didn't know a hell of a lot about cable television. I just knew more than anybody else in the area at that time. Not long after that, a man who had the franchise for Mankato got the franchise for Rochester and contacted me to build the system for him. That company's name was Rochester Video, Inc.—it was later sold to another group of Minnesota investors—and I supervised their engineering activities. Jack Kent Cooke acquired our company in the spring of 1965, and in June he moved me to his Beverly Hills offices, where I became his director of engineering. Within two weeks, he made me vice president of engineering, and in March 1966 I became the executive vice president of the company."

Although it wasn't until September 1970 that Bill came to Teleprompter (through a series of mergers headed by Jack Cooke), his association with Cooke in 1965 was the actual start of his career with his present corporation.

"Joining Mr. Cooke was the turning point in my career," Bill recalls with pride. "Jack is the greatest salesman in the world, bar none. He is also one of the smartest businessmen alive. Spending a year with him is a real education. I've been real lucky. I have had twelve years with him now."

Today, an estimated 3,700 cable television systems in the United States serve approximately 13 million subscribers. Teleprompter has 110 systems and an estimated 10 percent of the nation's total subscribers. It is the largest cable television company in the country—twice the size of the number two company.

Much of Teleprompter's success is due to its selling philosophy. *"We find a need, and then we respond to it,"* Bill emphasizes. "In my opinion, if you can do that, selling becomes easy. It all begins when we initially plan building a cable system.

We must first determine what services television viewers are presently getting in that community. Next, we figure what we can give them that they can't get without us. I refer to this difference as the *margin of service*. The wider that margin is, the easier it is to sell our service. If that margin is very narrow, in other words, if they can get very little extra with cable TV versus what is available without cable, well, then it's going to be a tough sale!

"Let me backtrack and explain how the cable TV business came to be. There were many small communities in the country where people could not get television without cable. The whole industry grew out of need. People living in outlying communities had to depend on a cable system to provide them with television. For example, in my hometown of Mankato, which is located about seventy miles down river from the Minneapolis–St. Paul area, until we put towers that were thirty to forty feet high up on the rooftops, we couldn't get any reception. And, even with those tall towers, we still got snow and poor reception. So when cable TV made excellent reception possible, it was a classic example of responding to a community's needs.

"Nowadays, a community like Mankato can get better reception than in the old days, but it's still not real good, so there's still a large margin of service in a community like that. But clearly we must plan our system from the very beginning and determine what we can give them that they don't already get. This means we must find out exactly what channels they're getting, what network service, which independent and educational channels. We must know exactly what kind of programming services they're getting, and likewise the quality of the signals they receive. Again, what can we give them that they can't get without us? Once we know this, our selling is easy! It's simply a matter of doing our homework right at the beginning.

"I don't think that our selling is nearly as hard as selling, for example, a product like cornflakes," Bill reflects. "Everybody has a need for breakfast, but I would hate to sell cornflakes if there were four or five different brands selling the same cereal. I consider that hard selling because I'd have to convince people that they should buy my cornflakes instead of four or five identical products. When we're selling a cable TV service to a community, we can offer them something which is essentially different from our competition in terms of services, the capacity of our system, the number of channels we carry, and certain rights we have to programs which we originate and create.

"Today, we have a track record, and that's important when we're selling our company to a community. When we're negotiating with a city council— you must remember that these are elected officials who also have needs we must respond to. Above all, they need to look good to the public. They can't afford to grant a franchise to some fly-by-night outfit that's not going to perform. You see, their reputations are on the line, and they have to do the best thing for the city. They must be convinced that Teleprompter has an outstanding track record. We have the engineering ability, the marketing ability, and the financial ability, and we're going to do a real professional job so the people will get good service. Elected officials don't want customers complaining and people storming into city hall. When voters shout, 'Where the hell did you get that lousy outfit you gave us?' that's very embarrassing for a politician.

"Like I said, we find the need and then we respond to it. All of this goes into planning the system, and once we've sold the city council that they should grant the franchise to us instead of to other companies, then we must build the system and sell the service to the public. I think that this selling is easy because we've planned properly, and we know that we have a product which is needed. As for trying to sell something that people don't need, I call that hustling—which is another profession altogether. That's not selling. It's very important for us to believe in what we offer the public. So we must know that we have something which they can't get without us!"

Once the franchise has been approved and the system has been built, Teleprompter must sell the service to the subscribers in the community. A strong emphasis is placed on penetrating the market, and today cable television companies are placing more stress on this facet of the business than on establishing new franchises. As Bill explains, "During the late sixties and early seventies, the cable TV industry was really flying high and people thought it was going to radically alter society. Everybody was trying to figure out ways that it would greatly improve the quality of American life. Everyone got into the act, including the regulators, social engineers, think-tankers, and do-gooders from all sorts of governmental agencies at all levels. Even the educators were seeking out all the marvelous services that the cable system could provide. Unfortunately, a lot of things which they contemplated were just not practical with the small operating base that the industry had. And often cable systems were built in large markets—in some of these our margin of service wasn't as wide as it should have been. Consequently, customers didn't come on as fast as capital was being invested. The problem was compounded when the prime rate rose to 12 percent, because we're in a very capital-intensive business. Fortunately we and other cable companies were able to cut back and regroup.

"Well," Bill says with a sigh of relief, "That's all behind us now. We've tightened our belts and trimmed the fat. We had to slow down in areas where we felt we couldn't provide as large a margin of service as we believed ought to be offered. Teleprompter is now back in good health. The entire industry has recovered fairly well, and it's just now starting to get out into the franchising business again. But we're not building new systems at the rapid pace of the past. We're concentrating more on communities where we're already doing business."

Because cable TV is a service business, Bill believes that it's important for everybody in the company to be service-oriented. "We gear all of our employees to be fully aware of servicing the customer," Bill emphasizes. "Everybody is constantly being instructed to serve. While something might seem like a minor thing, such as a technician or an installer taking off his muddy shoes before he enters a customer's home, don't for a second think that's not selling. He's showing that customer that *he cares,* and you have to instruct your people to react that way—you can't take it for granted.

"Another prime example of how our people do day-to-day selling is in how we instruct our telephone operators to handle incoming calls. It's very important for them to know how to deal with a customer who calls in with a complaint, or another one who may want to disconnect his service. Every telephone operator has what we call our 'bible.' This is a book which is broken down into sections and gives advice on how to handle an incoming call. Whether it's a disgruntled customer or an inquiry about a possible installation, our bible has a section on how to handle the situation.

"It doesn't matter what the problem is, we list it in the bible." Bill smiles. "Perhaps the caller feels he can't afford our service anymore, or he may be dissatisfied with the reception. Whatever it is, our operator can quickly turn to the index and find how how to handle that call. Many times a company will only have one contact with that caller, and if it's not handled properly the first time, there's not going to be another opportunity. So we have to satisfy that customer, and, of course, be ready to sell to a potential customer."

A concerned look appears on Bill's face. "A while ago, we had a system in an area where there seemed to be some public relations problems. For some reason, we had an image in that community as a company that didn't care. Of course we did care, but over a period of years we gradually appeared to have taken the attitude of a utility company. You know, 'We're the only cable company in town.' Well, that's a dangerous image to have. In order to reverse the deteriorating situation, we had our system manager take the door off the hinges of his office. That's right, actually *remove the door of his office!* We had the newspapers come in, and they took a picture of our manager taking the door off, and the article read something like 'Teleprompter manager's door is always open to the public.' We published the night line number of his office—the private line that bypassed the switchboard—and everyone was told to call him if they had any problems. Well, our manager loved it. He came up with most of the ideas himself! Of course, we had to have that kind of enthusiasm on his part, or the campaign wouldn't have worked. He and everybody else at the system answered the phone, 'Good morning, this is Teleprompter, the company that cares.' Well, through little things like that, we turned the poor image of the company around. It's surprising that not a whole lot of people called, but knowing that he cared enough to put his private phone number in the papers impressed the people.

"When I first joined Teleprompter," Bill continues, "I noticed that many of our system managers had their home telephone numbers unlisted, since they didn't want to receive complaints or crank calls at home. I put out a directive that said if they wanted to work for us, they had to be available. They now have their phone numbers listed, and, of course, *so is mine!* People have to know that we're accessible. Our managers can't be locked up in some isolation chamber. I believe that this availability is very crucial for a service company."

In 1974, Teleprompter introduced a new "pay cable" service in three New York City suburbs and in Los Angeles. The company had an encouraging response, and in 1975 entered into an agreement with Home Box Office (HBO), a subsidiary of Time Inc., which is capable of providing pay cable programming to all Teleprompter systems desiring it. HBO pay cable service offers many advantages such as uninterrupted and uncut first-run movies, sporting events, and other special programming which had not been previously available. Basic cable services cost from seven to ten dollars per month, and for HBO there is a similar charge.

Since the introduction of HBO, Teleprompter has made a concentrated effort to sell both services to their customers. Recently, new combination sales have been running 40 percent to 50 percent, but in the beginning, only about 15 percent of the customers bought both services. Company officials thought that a higher percentage of the basic cable customers should also take HBO,

and an all-out company effort was made to increase HBO sales.
"One of our managers did an experiment," Bill recalls, "and he
did it on his own, which is typical of the kind of spirit that we try
to create at our system level. Our local manager had a meeting
with his office people and told them he wanted them to sell HBO
services to 50 percent of all basic sales received on the telephone.
He told them that the first person to do it would receive a twenty-
five dollar gift certificate from a local dress shop. As part of the
effort, the manager made sure that everybody was fully familiar
with the program guide, and after he had carefully explained it to
them, they were really excited about HBO. He got them very
enthused, and pretty soon it was everybody's favorite topic of
conversation. At the end of the first month, they didn't average
50 percent, not one of them reached it, but they did average 30
percent. The sellers were disappointed and asked him to give
them another thirty-day contest.

"The second month, they averaged 52 percent!" Bill enthuses.
"I want you to know that that system is now averaging around 60
percent. But it was all because of the excitement that the manager
created. And in any of our systems, I don't care if it's a technician, a secretary, or the billing clerk—everyone has to know
what's on Home Box Office. They must know what's on every
program. It's that kind of involvement and enthusiasm that will
generate sales.

"I can't stress strongly enough how important it is for our
people to be fully aware of our programming. Each of our systems has door-to-door salespersons who must know the programming inside out. As in any kind of selling, it's imperative for
the salesman to listen carefully, and once he develops a comfortable rapport with the customer, and if he's at all responsive, he
should get a clue as to what the customer's needs are. If the
customer is interested in sports, for example, the salesman will
zero in on those needs and expand on the availability of basket-
ball, football, or whatever his customer's interest is. If the interest is movies, he'll mention all the first-run movies which are

going to be shown, and of course if he's selling Home Box Office, he'll stress that the movies are uninterrupted by commercials.

"HBO has opened up some new markets for our basic cable service. We knew, for example, that certain neighborhoods had always been better than others. We found our sales formed a bell curve: we weren't selling the low-income people or the wealthy; the middle-income people were our best market. Now that Home Box Office is available, the higher-income folks are buying, the ones with a higher lifestyle. These people are entertainment-oriented, so they're interested in the first-run movies and our HBO specials. We did an analysis to determine how to market our Home Box Office better. We correlated information about lifestyles, spendable incomes, educational levels, professions, and similar factors with zip-code maps of different communities. Well, once we were able to zero in on where HBO could be sold, we began to sell both the basic service and HBO to what had formerly been a weak market."

One of Bill's major activities is his work with Teleprompter's cable television system managers who are located throughout the country. "I believe that we must get our system managers totally involved in selling," Bill stresses. "As a matter of fact, over the last several years, I've concentrated very heavily on culling out the managers who weren't sales-oriented and, if necessary, replacing them. We're continually making an effort to upgrade the sales awareness of our managers.

"Some of them consider themselves administrators. You know, sort of like watchdogs over expenses. Sure, those things are important, but the really important thing is to bring the revenue in. We have a routine way of monitoring our costs and installations and trouble calls. It's all mechanized. If we have any trouble in those areas, we generally don't have any difficulties solving the problem. The big area, where the system managers must be strong, is in *getting sales*. That's where the dollars are. So we want our system managers to be sales managers. We expect them to get out into their territories. They're required to see their customers, and we want them to do some selling in order for them to understand what's going on in the field.

"And we don't expect a system manager to just make a call now and then. We expect him to do it on a routine basis. Everyone, from *myself* on down, goes out and knocks on doors. *I can learn more by knocking on doors during a four-hour period than I can learn in a three-year period sitting in my office!*

"I'll surprise a system by visiting them unexpectedly, and then tell the manager that I want to spend some time out in the field with a salesman. I guess the word gets out now, because they seem to know in advance that I'm coming." Bill grins. "I'll sit in on a sales meeting before the salespeople go out that evening, and I'll just pick out a guy, or perhaps a gal, and tell that person I want to spend the evening in the field with him or her. I tell them to introduce me as a trainee or as somebody who works for the company, but never as the company's president or a boss. I want to listen to what the customers think about Teleprompter. I am vitally concerned with our image, and their opinion of our service. I also get a good idea about how good a job we did in educating the public about cable television.

"Generally, I'll just keep quiet and do a lot of listening. I am particularly interested in calling on former customers who were unhappy with our service. You just can't imagine how much I learn about our operation when I get an opportunity to go out and talk candidly with people in their homes, present customers, non-customers, and former customers. The regional managers who work under me are required to make calls, and as for anyone in the organization who thinks he's too good to knock on doors—we don't need him!

"Not too long ago, I was visiting our Reno operation, and I told the system's sales manager that I wanted to go out selling that night. Well, it was a Friday afternoon, and he said, 'Gee, Bill, you live in New York, and the weekend is coming up. Do you mean that you want to stay here tonight and sell?' Not only was he flabbergasted, but he was absolutely thrilled that I would go out knocking on doors with him. When we got back to the office for a sales meeting around ten-thirty, all of his salespeople were there turning in their orders and having coffee. His excitement over having me show an interest by going out in the field with him had rubbed off, and all of his people got excited. They couldn't get over the fact that I was willing to spend time with their sales manager and fly home on Saturday morning rather than late Friday afternoon.''

It's no wonder that Teleprompter's system managers are willing to go out and see the people in their territories. If Bill Bresnan, the president of America's largest cable television company, can do it, so can they!

Cable television is a growing industry, and within the next decade it will offer many services in addition to its present ones. "We were just an antenna reception service when we started the business," Bill explains. "But now we're into pay TV with both a movie channel and with sports events. We're hoping soon to offer a children's pay channel which will have special programming for young people. and not only will it be a high-quality, wholesome product without sex and violence, but children won't be exploited by commercials, which, incidentally, many parents nowadays object to.

"And someday there will be a performing arts channel," Bill muses. "Maybe, each night we'll take the customer to one of the country's different cultural centers, like New York, Boston, or Philadelphia for a symphony or perhaps an opera. In other words, we can envision ourselves almost like a bookstore. Where one person may come in to buy one book, another individual might buy two or more. *Again, we're responding to the need.*''

11

A Final Message from the Author

As word got around that I was interviewing ten greatest salespersons, something totally unexpected happened. I was besieged by people wanting to know *What are these super salespersons like?* While I had anticipated reasonably high interest within selling circles, I was completely amazed by the fascination shared by everyone—not just salespeople.

After carefully analyzing this incredible general concern, I concluded three things: First, everyone, to some degree, sells. Second, everyone has been sold to. And finally, there is a special mystique about super salespersons.

The fact that everyone sells or is sold is nothing new; it simply illustrates that everyone has an instant identification with selling. It's the *mystique factor,* I believe, which accounts for the great amount of attention. I compare it to the magnetism and drawing power of America's modern hero, the NFL quarterback, or in previous times, the fascination stirred by the presence of a gunfighter of the Old West. To many, such comparisons may sound preposterous, but explore this analogy a few steps further. Americans are hero worshipers, and those individuals whom we place on the highest pedestals are the ones who perform super feats. Why? Because they're the *best!* Consider for a moment how much higher a salary a .300 baseball player can demand than a .200 player, yet the difference in their performance is only one extra hit in every ten times at bat! Likewise, the world's fastest human may only run the hundred-yard dash a fraction of a second faster than other runners.

However, there are vast differences in performances of salespeople. Within any company, the sales representatives will tend to have similar employment backgrounds, they receive the same training program, they're generally given similar territories, and they sell the same product. Although all of these factors are equal, it's general knowledge that 20 percent of all salespeople make 80 percent of the sales. Immediately, these disproportionate figures inform us that *a salesperson in the top 20 percent sells at a rate sixteen times higher than the rate of salesmen in the lower 80 percent.*

Probably the best example of someone who is definitely in a class by himself is Joe Gandolfo, who has sold $1 billion of life insurance in a single year. While the life insurance industry considers it a good year when a single individual sells $1 million, it would require a thousand such individuals to equal Joe's personal production! Similarly, Joe Girard sold 1,425 cars and trucks in a single year. Many large automobile agencies throughout the United States don't approach Joe's personal annual sales. And Martin Shafiroff generates approximately $1.5 million in annual commissions as a retail stockbroker. That, too, is a superhuman feat! Each of the other salespeople in this book is performing at a similar level; however, only in automobile, insurance, and securities sales is there a clear-cut measure for comparing these sales representatives' record-breaking results with achievements of others. People are amazed at these achievements, and for good reason!

For the remainder of this book, I will point out the common denominators among the ten greatest salespersons. First, I'm totally sold on them. Each of them is charming, personable, and delightful to be with. Although they are highly successful, they are also humble. There is absolutely no indication that their successes made them vain and egotistical, which sometimes happens with superstars.

Perhaps their most obvious common quality is their *love for selling*. I sincerely doubt whether any of them would have achieved his or her remarkable success in selling with a different attitude. I could sense enthusiasm and excitement in the air as I talked to each of them, and I am sure that their customers and clients must also feel it. Shelby Carter, Xerox's U.S. marketing vice president, doesn't have to make sales presentations in the field, but he declares, ''I enjoy going out and seeing customers, and to this day, I keep in touch . . . going out in the trenches with my troops. I call on customers across the country. It's something I love, and I'll continue to do it as long as I'm involved in marketing.''

Bill Bresnan, Teleprompter's president, also goes out in the field with his salesmen, on a door-to-door basis. Bill is so wrapped up in his work, you can feel his enthusiasm when he smiles. ''I can't think of any business I would rather be in than the cable television business.''

Blended so smoothly with their enthusiasm for selling is a *strong conviction* that they are offering the finest value to the customer. Joe Gandolfo feels that you must believe in it 100 percent. ''Do you know what? Before I owned a million on my own life, I couldn't sell a million, because I didn't see how anyone could afford it.'' The same philosophy applied as Joe advanced to selling several million dollars' worth of life insurance to his clients.

Edna Larsen matter-of-factly remarks, ''I believe in my products 100 percent, and my sincerity has to come across to my girls, so then they believe in Avon too.'' It only takes a few minutes talking with her to know exactly how powerful her sincerity really is.

And Martin Shafiroff states that if a client does not accept his investment concept, he will suggest that the client do business with somebody else. "If I don't, I'll lose my conviction," Martin explains. He maintains that without his "conviction factor," he would only be a mediocre salesman.

Bernice Hansen believes in her Amway products so strongly that she attributes her self-confidence to this belief. "You know," she says, "people can *sense* this kind of confidence, and you've got to have it in order to be effective in selling." She adds that to this day she uses the food supplement products she sold in the early 1950s when Amway was still a dream.

Along with possessing convictions about the product, most of these salespeople place a strong emphasis on *product knowledge*. Rich Port built one of the nation's most successful residential real estate firms because, as he explains, "I was determined to be a professional and accumulate all the knowledge available on real estate." That attitude is reflected in the highly professional sales staff of Rich Port, Realtor.

Mike Curto tells how a salesman will be moved through US Steel's different mills and be exposed to all facets of the steel industry during the course of several years. "We're trying to get our people oriented to the total business venture," he explains, so that they can make proper decisions.

Perhaps Buck Rodgers gets the message across best when he reveals that IBM has training centers located throughout the United States and in fifty foreign countries. With a smile, he says, "We're figuratively the largest university in the world!"

Because so many demands are made upon them, each places an extremely high value on time. Without question, effective time management is a high priority among all successful people. Edna Larsen believes that her success in selling Avon Products is due to her vast exposure to her customers compared to the average salesperson. While others spend less than 25 percent of their time eyeball-to-eyeball with customers, she is spending more than 90 percent of her time with them.

Martin Shafiroff keeps a formula on his desk that gives him "direction on where I should be going and what I should be doing." He further explains that the average stockbroker is in contact with customers only thirty minutes of his selling time each day. "If I can increase it to four or five hours, well . . . the leverage involved is quite dramatic." Martin manages his time so efficiently that he is able to average sixty telephone calls to his clients and prospects on a typical working day!

And Joe Girard refers to his time-management plan with "I get the most out of my 1,440." I must confess that it took me a while to figure out there are 1,440 minutes in a twenty-four-hour period!

Rich Port believes in utilizing time efficiently so much that he suggests that his associates take a different route to work each day to find out what's going on in the area. He has even written a pamphlet for his staff titled *24 Things to Do When You Think There Is Nothing to Do.*

Listening to the customer isn't normally a priority for most salespeople; however, the ten greatest are all *people who listen.* Joe Gandolfo believes that the warm-up session he conducts with each prospect is the embodiment of his philosophy that "selling is 98 percent understanding human beings and 2 percent product knowledge." Joe states, "Asking a lot of questions and doing a lot of listening, well, that's the best way to understand people." Even his office walls attest to his listening philosophy: one plaque reads, "God gave you two ears and one mouth, and He meant for you to do twice as much listening as talking."

On occasion, Bill Bresnan will sell door-to-door with one of Teleprompter's cable television salesmen because "I can learn more by knocking on doors during a four-hour period than I can learn in a three-year period sitting in my office!" He claims he just sits back and observes. "I want to listen to what the customers think about Teleprompter. . . . Generally, I'll just keep quiet and do a lot of listening."

Throughout the ten interviews, each salesperson claimed that *servicing the customer* is a highly important part of selling. Mike Curto believes that service is essential in selling steel. He suggests that since on the surface "there's not a great deal to sell, because the differences in our product and our competitor's seem so insignificant, we *have* to sell service."

Joe Girard believes this too. He says, "The sale really begins after the sale—not before! When the customer comes back for service, I fight for him all the way to get him the best. . . . I really go to bat for him."

And Buck Rodgers says, "We have good reason to say, 'IBM means service.' We're dealing with a customer on a continuing basis . . . and unless we continue to give the customer the best possible service, always looking out for his best interest, we take the risk of losing him." He smiles confidently as he adds, "We have the capacity to respond to a problem in any part of the world."

Along with servicing, there were several comments about establishing a special *relationship with the customer*. Rich Port believes that "the salesman who establishes the proper relationship with his client, the seller, will discover that, in essence, it's the finest relationship that exists in the business world. You should consider it a partnership."

Buck Rodgers has a similar message for selling computers. "At IBM we think it's important that a partnership be developed so the customer realizes there's something more than just a one-time-call situation. Over a period of time, the salesman can go in and develop an understanding of the customer, so that the salesman can put together a plan that has substance over a several-year period."

US Steel also develops a close relationship with its customers over a period of time. "US Steel has more than a thousand people in its research group," Mike Curto states. "We take our technical people right to the customer's plant, so they get to know the manufacturing people, and they all become very closely associated. It's really a team effort. And we like for our customers to think of us as being on the same team. We're working with them to solve problems the customer is having in manufacturing."

And while these ten great salespersons do all of the major facets of selling just right, they also *look after the small details*. A good example of this is Joe Girard sending out his monthly "I like you" letters. He never takes a phone call while he's with a customer. And Joe has heart-shaped balloons and lollipops for the customers' children. He even has a full bar of whiskey for the customer who "needs a drink." He stocks all kinds of cigarettes! He always makes sure to give each customer a handful of business cards, which say, "Enjoy the thrill of a good deal." Yes, Joe believes in the "little things" that every automobile salesman may know about. *The difference is that Joe does them!*

Rich Port never misses a selling point, no matter how small. He explains that he would never pull into a driveway with a potential buyer, but would approach the home by parking down the street, because it's important that the buyer approach the home for the first time from the most advantageous view. And Rich is probably the only salesman I ever met who jotted down the *dog's name*. As he tells it, "Boy, I'll tell you that when people are nice to my dog and call him by his right name, I like it." So Rich figures that his customers like it when he's nice to their dog!

Martin Shafiroff also is very much aware of getting the proper name—he jots down the name of his client's secretary. And the next time he calls, he addresses her by name. While this may sound like a minor point, Martin is convinced that it's very effective, since the secretary often must screen her employer's calls.

Although IBM is a very large corporation by anyone's standards, Buck Rodgers insists that IBM salespeople take care of details. "It's equally important to tend to the little things, like attending meetings on time. Or perhaps a customer asked for some information, maybe some brochures. Well, the salesperson better make it his business to see that the customer gets what he asked for. Another little thing which too many salespeople neglect to do is to promptly return calls from their customers. These things help develop a relationship of mutual trust."

The little things! I would venture to say that none of these ten salespersons overlooks a single detail in his or her selling effort. As they say in show business, "He really put his act together." After each interview, I could only describe each individual by saying, "He (or she) really knows his business. He's a real pro!" And I firmly believe that a truly professional person doesn't allow a thing, no matter how insignificant, to go unattended. This is especially true of the top person in a particular field. The competition is too keen—and it requires that "extra effort" to be number one.

If there were any weaknesses in the ten greatest salespersons, I didn't discover them. Each of them was strong in all areas of salesmanship. It wasn't as though an individual could have strengths in one area that would overcompensate for a weakness in another. Each of them functioned with perfection; they are completely aware of how they sell, and each action has a clear reason. They don't happen by chance to sell the way they do. And each time they sell, they strive for excellence. It's a matter of pride.

Ten Greatest Salespersons is a collection of thoughts and selling techniques that illustrate how the best sales talent in America gets results. It extends an unequaled opportunity to the reader to learn from the best. It offers exposure to the ideas of super sales personalities who work in various industries. And again, I strongly emphasize the enormous value of learning about how selling is done in fields that are different from your own.

Finally, as I completed the ten interviews, in addition to being asked, "What are these ten greatest salespersons like?" people began to ask me, "Who is your favorite?" and "Who is the *greatest* salesperson?" How do you compare an Amway representative with a cable television executive, a securities salesman with an automobile salesman, or a steel executive with a copier executive?

Frankly, I don't think you can determine *who the best is*. It reminds me of Napoleon's reply to Madame Montholon when she inquired which troops he considered the best. "Those which are victorious, Madame," the emperor answered.

The Ten Greatest Salespersons are all victorious.

About the Author

ROBERT L. SHOOK has had a successful sales career since his graduation from Ohio State University in 1959. He is chairman of the board of American Executive Corporation and the author of *Winning Images, How to Be the Complete Professional Salesman* (with Herbert M. Shook), and *Total Commitment* (with Ronald Bingamen). He lives in Columbus, Ohio, with his wife and three children.